his tail's

The twos

sence, the

true fury! Behold

the sun father

! Long may he
100

ON THE POET
AND HIS CRAFT

Selected Prose of Theodore Roethke

ON THE POET
AND HIS CRAFT

Selected Prose of Theodore Roethke

Edited with an Introduction by Ralph J. Mills, Jr.

University of Washington Press
Seattle and London, 1965

ACKNOWLEDGMENTS

PART ONE. "Some Self-Analysis," a student essay, was one of a number Roethke wrote at the University of Michigan and was probably composed during his sophomore year, 1926-27. "An American Poet Introduces Himself and His Poems" was presented as a BBC broadcast, July 30, 1953 (Disc #SLO 34254). "Theodore Roethke" is from *Twentieth Century Authors, First Supplement*, edited by Stanley J. Kunitz (New York: H. W. Wilson, 1955), pp. 837-38. "On 'Identity' " was a statement made at a Northwestern University panel on "Identity" in February, 1963.

PART TWO. "Verse in Rehearsal" is from *Portfolio* (Pennsylvania State University), Vol. 1 (September,

1939), pp. 3, 15-16. "Open Letter" appeared originally in *Mid-Century American Poets*, edited by John Ciardi (New York: Twayne, 1950), pp. 67-72. "The Teaching Poet" is from *Poetry*, LXXIX (February, 1952), 250-55. "A Word to the Instructor," written in 1954, was originally intended as the introductory piece for the anthology *Twelve Poets*, edited by Glenn Leggett. The publishers of the anthology, however, decided against including it; therefore, this piece is published here for the first time. "Theodore Roethke Writes . . ." appeared originally in the *Poetry Book Society Bulletin* (London), No. 16, December, 1957. "How to Write Like Somebody Else" is from the *Yale Review*, XLVIII (March, 1959), 336-43. First publication of "Some Remarks on Rhythm" was in *Poetry*, XCVII (October, 1960), 35-46.

PART THREE. "One Ring-Tailed Roarer to Another" is from *Poetry*, LXXXI (December, 1952), 184-86. It was signed by the pseudonym, Winterset Rothberg. "Dylan Thomas: Elegy" was a part of "Dylan Thomas: Memories and Appreciations" from *Encounter*, II (January, 1954), 11. "Richard Selig" was part of "Tribute to Richard Selig—1929-1957" in *Gemini: Oxford and Cambridge Magazine*, I (Winter, 1957-58), 62-63. "Last Class," under the pseudonym Winterset Rothberg, appeared first in *Botteghe Oscure* (Rome), V (1950), 400-406; it was reprinted in *College English*, XVIII (May, 1957), 383-86. (Thanks are due to the Honorable Mrs. Hubert Howard [Lelia Caetani], acting for the late Princess Marguerite Caetani di Sermoneta, for permission to reprint.)

PART FOUR. The review of *The Last Look and Other Poems* by Mark Van Doren is from the *New Republic*, XCIII (Nov. 17, 1937), 52. The review of *And Spain*

Sings: Fifty Loyalist Ballads is from *Poetry*, LII (April, 1938), 43-46. The review of Ben Belitt's *The Five-Fold Mesh* appeared in *Poetry*, LIII (January, 1939), 214-17. The review of *Concerning the Young* by Willard Maas is from *Poetry*, LIII (March, 1939), 336-38. The review of *The Alert* by Wilfred Gibson and *Gautama the Enlightened* by John Masefield appeared in *Poetry*, LX (May, 1942), 109-10. The review of Roy Fuller's *A Lost Season* is from *Poetry*, LXVII (January, 1946), 218-21. The review of *The Earth-Bound* by Janet Lewis is from *Poetry*, LXIX (January, 1947), 220-23. "Five American Poets" is an introduction to selections from the poetry of Stanley Kunitz, Jean Garrigue, Chester Kallman, David Wagoner, and Roethke himself. It is from *New World Writing* (Fourth Mentor Selection, 1953), pp. 83-85. "The Poetry of Louise Bogan" is from the *Critical Quarterly* (Summer, 1961), pp. 142-50.

EPILOGUE. Published posthumously under the pseudonym Winterset Rothberg, "A Tirade Turning" originally appeared in *Encounter*, XXI (December, 1963), 44-45.

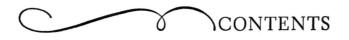CONTENTS

Introduction   xi

PART ONE

Some Self-Analysis   3
An American Poet Introduces Himself
    and His Poems   7
Theodore Roethke   14
On "Identity"   18

PART TWO

Verse in Rehearsal   31
Open Letter   36
The Teaching Poet   44
A Word to the Instructor   52
Theodore Roethke Writes . . .   57
How to Write Like Somebody Else   61
Some Remarks on Rhythm   71

PART THREE

One Ring-Tailed Roarer to Another — 87
Dylan Thomas: Elegy — 90
Richard Selig — 93
Last Class — 96

PART FOUR

Reviews — 107
Five American Poets — 129
The Poetry of Louise Bogan — 133

EPILOGUE

A Tirade Turning — 151

INTRODUCTION

AMONG THE IMPORTANT POETS OF OUR CENTURY FEW HAVE avoided altogether the writing of essays or lectures, critical prose. For some—T. S. Eliot and Ezra Pound spring immediately to mind as perhaps the most obvious examples—the efforts in prose were calculated to clear the ground for their poetry: a necessary maneuver because that poetry was new and experimental, radical in conception and execution, and it required the education of a taste by which it could be appreciated. The case of William Butler Yeats is something else again. We find the entire, wide range of his interests—in Irish folklore, politics, and the theater; in mysticism and the occult; in poetry and symbolism; in his own life, the friends, circumstances, and preoccupations which shaped it—taking its full share in the production of his prose. On the other hand, the prose of Wallace Stevens seems simply an extension of the thought, the metaphysical enterprise informing his poetry but stripped of the poetry's linguistic elegance and metaphorical richness, though often compensating for this with an aphoristic precision.

The prose writings which Theodore Roethke left behind him at his death in August, 1963, hardly differ from those of the other poets I have mentioned in consisting almost exclusively of occasional pieces: book reviews, prefaces and introductions, broadcasts, university lectures, statements about his own work or autobiographical remarks for a reference book, parodies and satires. Roethke was not, however, nor is it likely that he would have become had he lived another twenty-five or thirty years, a poet who was also a critical theorist, who proposed some new departure from existing poetic forms in which all writers should participate or who announced a movement that would revolutionize literature. Yet he was, as even the lightest perusal of his poems will amply demonstrate, a writer who, in the practical sphere, carried out—and how beautifully and successfully too!—some of the most astonishing experiments in the history of modern verse. At the same time, he maintained, as the other side of his poetic endeavor, a commitment to the traditional lyric as it has been practiced from the Elizabethans to Yeats, and on to Stanley Kunitz and Louise Bogan. While Roethke's prose sets forth neither programs nor theories, it does provide, again and again, in explanations of purpose with regard to his own work, and in discussion and judgment of the work of others, his fundamental aims and his beliefs about the art of poetry. Though his prose pieces are miscellaneous, not usually ordered to any end beyond the subject at hand, and sometimes repeat one another slightly, they have the advantage of being perhaps truer and of greater authenticity because they lack the self-consciousness or the rhetorical motives which often mar more theoretical statements.

Roethke's prose, from the early reviews of Mark Van Doren, Spanish loyalist poets, and others, to his later and more personal pieces such as "Open Letter" or "Some Remarks on Rhythm," is always instantaneously recognizable as that of a working poet who takes his vocation very seriously indeed. The identifying mark in this respect is, I believe, a constant, unflagging attention to matters of craft and form, the fundamentals of the poem on which everything else is built and depends. And when he is not discussing such details with reference to Ben Belitt or Louise Bogan, he is doing so in writing about literary influences on his own poetry ("How to Write Like Somebody Else") or in treating some of the many problems which confront the teacher of poetry ("A Word to the Instructor") and the poet-teacher who conducts a workshop course in the composition of verse ("The Teaching Poet"). Again, Roethke's concern with these affairs is not theoretical or purely speculative; he was as concretely aware as any poet could be of the forces molding his work, stirring his imagination; and he was a teacher of many years' experience, as well as of legendary reputation. For him, the making of a poem by an individual, a student, the honesty, tenacity, labor of craftsmanship it demanded, in addition to the gifts donated by the imagination, comprised a unique and worthy human act; whether the poem which resulted from it was a masterpiece or only a minor success was unimportant in comparison with what was attempted. We might point out here that a continuation of this attitude characterizes Roethke's valuations of other poets: he took little interest in literary fashion or critical reputation in estimating poetry; writers are not judged by their names, their innovations, their place in some invented hierarchy, but specifically, with the performance of each isolated poem.

In a number of essays and lectures, several heretofore unpublished, Roethke openly discusses his own poetry and portions of the background of experience from which it derived. When his many notebooks are edited and published, as they undoubtedly will be in the coming years, we shall learn much more about the development of this magnificent poet, and learn it in detail at the source. But for the purposes of his readers now, there is a good deal to be discovered and gained from attention to pieces like "Open Letter," in which the sequence poems of childhood from *The Lost Son* and *Praise to the End* are commented upon at length; "Some Remarks on Rhythm," which not only offers excellent statements about sound and rhythm in poetry but also points, in certain of its remarks, to the technique of the long, free lines, the "catalogue" use of descriptive detail, so prominent in the "North American Sequence" from *The Far Field*; and "An American Poet Introduces Himself and His Poems" and "On 'Identity,' " both of which supply interesting biographical material, indicate something of this poet's direction and his convictions. No one who has found Roethke's poetry to be rich and moving will, I believe, be disappointed by his prose. Once we have understood that the pieces included here were written for definite occasions, and that Roethke was not otherwise much given to expressing himself publicly in prose but devoted himself wholeheartedly to his poems, then we shall know how to approach them. Even his book reviews contain sharp, valuable observations, and we should be the poorer for not having them readily available. It is my hope that this small collection of Theodore Roethke's prose will stand on book shelves along with the volumes of his poetry, for these essays, lectures, and reviews are worth turning to repeatedly for the help they give us, deepening our insight into the work and adding to our minds from this fine poet's store of wisdom about poetic art.

I have divided this book into four sections. The first, which begins with a paper Roethke wrote as a student at the University of Michigan, includes several statements about his life and work. Section two is composed of various papers on the craft of poetry—on his own poems, aspects of poetry in general, and comments about the teaching of verse. Two memoirs, one of Dylan Thomas, another of Richard Selig, a young poet and former student of Roethke's, plus two extravagant prose pieces written under the pseudonym "Winterset Rothberg" make up a third part. Finally, in section four, I have placed most of Roethke's book reviews, as well as an introduction to a selection of poems by several contemporary poets and his full-length essay on Louise Bogan, whose work—like that of Léonie Adams, Stanley Kunitz, and Rolfe Humphries, among others—he so strongly admired. A late

"Winterset Rothberg" piece, posthumously published, appears as an epilogue.

I should like to offer here my warmest thanks to Beatrice Roethke, the poet's widow, for her initial suggestion that I edit this collection, and for her unfailing help and kindness. Miss Judith Johnson of the Manuscripts Section of the University of Washington library has aided me in many ways with information about papers and in handling matters of permissions. Mr. John W. Matheson's bibliography of Roethke has been of invaluable help in locating and identifying material. I should like to thank as well Mrs. Irving Gold for her typing of the manuscript of this book, and Mr. Maurice English for suggesting its title.

RALPH J. MILLS, JR.
University of Chicago

PART ONE

SOME SELF-ANALYSIS

I EXPECT THIS COURSE TO OPEN MY EYES TO STORY MATE-rial, to unleash my too dormant imagination, to develop that quality utterly lacking in my nature—a sense of form. I do not expect to acquire much technique. I expect to be able to seize upon the significant, reject the trivial. I hope to acquire a greater love for humanity in all its forms.

I have long wondered just what my strength was as a writer. I am often filled with tremendous enthusiasm for a subject, yet my writing about it will seem a sorry attempt. Above all, I possess a driving sincerity,—that prime virtue of any creative worker. I write only what I believe to be the absolute truth,—even if I must ruin the theme in so doing. In this respect I feel far superior to those glib people in my classes who often garner better grades than I do. They are so often pitiful frauds,—artificial—insincere. They have a line that works. They do not write from the depths of their hearts. Nothing of theirs was ever born of pain. Many an incoherent yet sincere piece of writing has outlived the polished product.

I write only about people and things that I know thoroughly. Perhaps I have become a mere reporter, not a writer. Yet I feel that this is all my present abilities permit. I will open my eyes in my youth and store this raw, living material. Age may bring the fire that molds experience into artistry.

I have a genuine love of nature. It is not the least bit affected, but an integral and powerful part of my life. I know that Cooper is a fraud—that he doesn't give a true sense of the sublimity of American scenery. I know that Muir and Thoreau and Burroughs speak the truth.

I can sense the moods of nature almost instinctively. Ever since I could walk, I have spent as much time as I could in the open. A perception of nature—no matter how delicate, how subtle, how evanescent,—remains with me forever.

I am influenced too much, perhaps, by natural objects. I seem bound by the very room I'm in. I've associated so long with prosaic people that I've dwarfed myself spiritually. When I get alone under an open sky where man isn't too evident,—then I'm tremendously exalted and a thousand vivid ideas and sweet visions flood my consciousness.

I think that I possess story material in abundance. I have had an unusual upbringing. I was let alone, thank God! My mother insisted upon two things,—that I strive for perfection in whatever I did and that I always try to be a gentleman. I played with Italians, with Russians, Poles, and the "sissies" on Michigan avenue. I was carefully watched, yet allowed to follow my own inclinations. I have seen a good deal of life that would never have been revealed to an older person. Up to the time I came to college then I had seen humanity in diverse forms. Now I'm cramped and unhappy. I don't feel that these idiotic adolescents are worth writing about. In the summer, I turn animal and work for a few weeks in a factory. Then I'm happy.

My literary achievements have been insignificant. At fourteen, I made a speech which was translated into twenty-six languages and used as Red Cross propaganda. When I was younger, it seemed that everything I wrote was eminently successful. I always won a prize when I entered an essay contest. In college, I've been able to get only one "A" in four rhetoric courses. I feel this keenly. If I can't write, what can I do? I wonder.

When I was a freshman, I told Carleton Wells that I knew I could write whether he thought so or not. On my next theme he wrote "You can Write!" How I have cherished that praise!

It is bad form to talk about grades, I know. If I don't get an "A" in this course, it wouldn't be because I haven't tried. I've made a slow start. I'm going to spend Christmas vacation writing. A "B" symbolizes defeat to me. I've been beaten too often.

I do wish that we were allowed to keep our stories until we felt that we had worked them into the best possible form.

I do not have the divine urge to write. There seems to

be something surging within,—a profound undercurrent of emotion. Yet there is none of that fertility of creation which distinguishes the real writer.

Nevertheless, I have faith in myself. I'm either going to be a good writer or a poor fool.

not creation; Word order

AN AMERICAN POET
INTRODUCES HIMSELF
AND HIS POEMS

EVERYONE KNOWS THAT AMERICA IS A CONTINENT, BUT FEW Europeans realize the various and diverse parts of this land. The Saginaw Valley, where I was born, had been great lumbering country in the 1880's. It is very fertile flat country in Michigan, and the principal towns, Saginaw and Flint, lie at the northern edge of what is now the central industrial area of the United States.

It was to this region that my grandfather came in 1870 from Prussia, where he had been Bismarck's head forester. He and his sons started some greenhouses which became the most extensive in that part of America.

It was a wonderful place for a child to grow up in and around. There were not only twenty-five acres in the town, mostly under glass and intensely cultivated, but farther out in the country the last stand of virgin timber in the Saginaw Valley and, elsewhere, a wild area of cut-over second-growth timber, which my father and uncle made into a small game preserve.

As a child, then, I had several worlds to live in, which I felt were mine. One favorite place was a swampy corner of the game sanctuary where herons always nested. I put down one of my earlier memories in a poem about them:

The heron stands in water where the swamp
Has deepened to the blackness of a pool,
Or balances with one leg on a hump
Of marsh grass heaped above a musk-rat hole.

He walks the shallow with an antic grace.
The great feet break the ridges of the sand,
The long eye notes the minnow's hiding place.
His beak is quicker than a human hand.

He jerks a frog across his bony lip,
Then points his heavy bill above the wood.
The wide wings flap but once to lift him up.
A single ripple starts from where he stood.

What the greenhouses themselves were to me I try to indicate in my second book, The Lost Son and Other Poems, published in this country [England] in 1949. They were to me, I realize now, both heaven and hell, a kind of tropics created in the savage climate of Michigan, where austere German-Americans turned their love of order and their terrifying efficiency into something truly

8

beautiful. It was a universe, several worlds, which, even as a child, one worried about, and struggled to keep alive, as in the poem "Big Wind":

> Where were the greenhouses going,
> Lunging into the lashing
> Wind driving water
> So far down the river
> All the faucets stopped?—
> So we drained the manure-machine
> For the steam plant,
> Pumping the stale mixture
> Into the rusty boilers,
> Watching the pressure gauge
> Waver over to red,
> As the seams hissed
> And the live steam
> Drove to the far
> End of the rose-house,
> Where the worst wind was,
> Creaking the cypress window-frames,
> Cracking so much thin glass
> We stayed all night,
> Stuffing the holes with burlap;
> But she rode it out,
> The old rose-house,
> She hove into the teeth of it,
> The core and pith of that ugly storm,
> Ploughing with her stiff prow,
> Bucking into the wind-waves
> That broke over the whole of her,
> Flailing her sides with spray,
> Flinging long strings of wet across the roof-top,
> Finally veering, wearing themselves out, merely

9

> *Whistling thinly under the wind-vents;*
> *She sailed until the calm morning,*
> *Carrying her full cargo of roses.*

In those first poems I had begun, like the child, with small things and had tried to make plain words do the trick. Somewhat later, in 1945, I began a series of longer pieces which try, in their rhythms, to catch the movement of the mind itself, to trace the spiritual history of a protagonist (not "I" personally but of all haunted and harried men); to make this sequence a true and not arbitrary order which would permit many ranges of feeling, including humor.

All these states of mind were to be rendered dramatically, without comment, without allusion, the action often implied or indicated in the interior monologue or dialogue between the self and its mentor, or conscience, or, sometimes, another person.

How to create a reality, a verisimilitude, the "as if" of the child's world, in language a child would use, was, for me, enormously difficult. For instance, the second poem, "I Need, I Need," opens with very oral imagery, the child's world of sucking and licking. Then there is a shift to a passage in which two children are jumping rope. The reader isn't *told* the children are jumping rope: he simply hears the two reciting, alternately, jingles to each other; then this mingled longing and aggressiveness changes, in the next passage, to a vaguely felt, but definite, feeling of love in one of the children:

1.

> *A deep dish. Lumps in it.*
> *I can't taste my mother.*

Hoo. *I know the spoon.*
Sit in my mouth.

A *sneeze can't sleep.*
Diddle we care
Couldly.

Went *down cellar,*
Talked to a faucet;
The drippy water
Had nothing to say.

Whisper *me over,*
Why don't you, begonia,
There's no alas
Where I live.

Scratched *the wind with a stick.*
The leaves liked it.
Do the dead bite?
Mamma, she's a sad fat.

A *dove said dove all day.*
A hat is a house.
I hid in his. . . .

3.

Stop *the larks. Can I have my heart back?*
Today I saw a beard in a cloud.
The ground cried my name:
Good-bye for being wrong.
Love helps the sun.
But not enough.

4.

When *you plant, spit in the pot.*
A pick likes to hit ice.

Hooray for me and the mice!—
The oats are all right.

Hear me, soft ears and roundy stones!
It's a dear life I can touch.
Who's ready for pink and frisk?
My hoe eats like a goat.

> *Her feet said yes.*
> *It was all hay.*
> *I said to the gate,*
> *Who else knows*
> *What water does?*
> *Dew ate the fire.*

I know another fire.
Has roots.

In the subsequent poems we hear the young adolescent, half a child, then the randy young man boasting and caterwauling; and finally more difficult passages in which the mind, under great stress, roves far back into the subconscious, later emerging into the "light" of more serene or euphoric passages at the end of each phase of experience.

Sometimes, of course, there is a regression. I believe that the spiritual man must go back in order to go forward. The way is circuitous, and sometimes lost, but invariably returned to.

Some of the technical devices characteristic of this sequence—the rapidly shifting metaphor, the rhetorical questions, and the like—reappear in more formal poems completed recently, entitled "Four for Sir John Davies," which are, among other things, a tribute to the Elizabethan author of "Orchestra" and to the late W. B. Yeats.

THE DANCE

Is that dance slowing in the mind of man
That made him think the universe could hum?
The great wheel turns its axle when it can;
I need a place to sing, and dancing-room,
And I have made a promise to my ears
I'll sing and whistle romping with the bears.

For they are all my friends: I saw one slide
Down a steep hillside on a cake of ice,—
Or was that in a book? I think with pride:
A caged bear rarely does the same thing twice
In the same way: O watch his body sway!—
This animal remembering to be gay.

I tried to fling my shadow at the moon,
The while my blood leaped with a wordless song.
Though dancing needs a master, I had none
To teach my toes to listen to my tongue.
But what I learned there, dancing all alone,
Was not the joyless motion of a stone.

I take this cadence from a man named Yeats;
I take it, and I give it back again:
For other tunes and other wanton beats
Have tossed my heart and fiddled through my brain.
Yes, I was dancing-mad, and how
That came to be the bears and Yeats would know.

THEODORE ROETHKE

I MIGHT MANAGE TO WRITE AN ANECDOTAL AND PERHAPS even semi-engaging and mildly witty account of my life; but of what importance is it that I grew up in and around a beautiful green-house owned by my father and uncle; that I hated high school and Michigan and Harvard (in spite of fine teachers like Strauss, Campbell, Rice, I. A. Richards and others); that I have taught in various colleges and coached tennis; worked in a pickle factory for several seasons; have lived, alternately, very quietly and then foolishly and violently; that I have been called "as good a steak cook as Brancusi" by William Carlos Williams; and that the kids at Bennington in a burst of misdirected generosity called me "the best teacher we ever had"; that my books have been treated with astonishing generosity by good critics and poets and the young; that the English seem to like me even better; and that I mean almost nothing (except for a handful of personal friends) to the people of my own state, to the man in the street—and desire that regard most passionately; that I am much interested in oral presentation.

All such details, and others like them, seem particularly trivial and vulgar in my case because I have tried to put them down in poems, as barely and honestly as possible, symbolically, what few nuggets of observation and, let us hope, spiritual wisdom I have managed to seize upon in the course of a conventional albeit sometimes disordered existence. I have tried to transmute and purify my "life," the sense of being defiled by it, in both small and formal and somewhat blunt short poems, and latterly, in longer poems which try in their rhythms to catch the very movement of the mind itself, to trace the spiritual history of a protagonist (not "I," personally), of all haunted and harried men; to make in this series (now probably finished) a true and not arbitrary order which will permit many ranges of feeling, including humor.

I began, like the child, with small things. I had no interest in verse after an intense period of pleasure in nursery rhymes in English and German and songs my mother and my nurse sang me. I really wanted, at fifteen and sixteen, to write a beautiful, a "chiseled" prose as it was called in those days. There were books at home and I went to the local libraries (and very good ones they were for such a smallish town); read Stevenson, Pater, Newman, Tomlinson, and those maundering English charm boys known as familiar essayists. I bought on my own editions of Emer-

son, Thoreau, and, as God's my witness, subscribed to the
Dial when I was in the seventh grade. I was strong for
anthologies of great thoughts, including Elbert Hubbard;
and had such deep interest in the short story that I started
buying the O'Brien anthologies in 1920 when I was
twelve. (You could make money in the short story!)

My first verses, and dreadful they were, I sold for $1.
About a year later when I was moping through the Harvard Yard one night, I saw a man I thought might be
Robert Hillyer. I said boldly, "Pardon me, Sir, I think I
have some poems you might like." A look of pain came
over his face. "Come to my office at eleven," he said. I
did, complete with fur coat and a fancy suit (those Harvards weren't going to have it over me!). Ushered in by
his secretary he took the verse, started reading. Suddenly
he wheeled in his chair. "Any editor who wouldn't buy
these is a fool!" he said. I was overwhelmed (though I
had thought so too!). There were only three poems, but
Ridgely Torrence of the *New Republic* and George Shuster, then of *Commonweal*, did buy two of them.

I felt I had come to the end (really the beginning) of a
trail. I had learned how to get high grades, but that
seemed meaningless. Now I didn't have to go into advertising (I had written at eighteen copy which had been
used in national campaigns), or the law. I wasn't just a
spoiled sad snob. I could write and people I respected
printed the stuff.

It took me ten years to complete one little book, and
now some of the things in it seem to creak. Still, I like
about ten pieces in it. Writers were extraordinarily generous to me in a very personal way in this long incubation,
particularly in what not to do. Let me name some:

W. H. Auden, Louise Bogan, Malcolm Cowley, Babette Deutsch, Rolfe Humphries, John Holmes, Stanley Kunitz, Douglas Moore, A. J. M. Smith, William Carlos Williams, and latterly, Kenneth Burke, Edith Sitwell, and many students. These people, maybe without realizing it, spoke with absolute candor and often with great insight; they often kept me from going down blind alleys or wasting what time I had for writing better.

I write this down because it is a matter rarely mentioned. I owe much less, I believe, to the *work* of contemporaries than to their qualities as men and women. And that debt is immense.

ON "IDENTITY"

I REMEMBER THE LATE E. E. CUMMINGS ONCE ANSWERED A questionnaire—from *New Verse*, the English magazine of the thirties: answered it by quotations from his own work. At the time, being a fierce, youngish man, I thought this a bit exhibitionistic: but now I'm beginning to see the point. One has said a thing as best one can in the poem—in usually a dramatic context: why debase it or water it down to a didactic prose for a lazy modern audience. But this is not a lazy audience, but a young, idealistic, and deeply serious audience: I can judge by its letters, its questions, indeed, I have been astonished at the pertinence, the relevance of the general subjects; and even more astonished by the fact that, I judge from Mr. Payson Wilde's letter, all this has official credence and sanction. It would seem you have administrators who read—even books.

I take it that we are faced with at least four principal themes: (1) The multiplicity, the chaos of modern life; (2) The way, the means of establishing a personal identity, a self in the face of that chaos; (3) The nature of creation, that faculty for producing order out of disorder in the arts, particularly in poetry; and (4) The nature of God Himself.

I take it as the poet, the intuitive man, I am entitled to, am expected to, throw out what suggestions, what hints I can from my own work, from my own life. I think of this life as an instrument, as an example; and I am perfectly willing to appear ridiculous, absurd, if a real point can be established, a real dent can be made.

I had reason to be delighted with Mr. Bracken's letter: after all he quoted from my work four times. An all-time record. "Nice young man," I thought; "either going to go far, or go entirely mad." Besides, his prose was better than mine. I felt that, in Kierkegaardian terms, we had reached the true state of education in one bound: the student was teaching the teacher. Behind his letter and the various statements I received, one could sense a real hunger for a reality more than the immediate: a desire not only for a finality, for a consciousness beyond the mundane, but a desire for quietude, a desire for joy. Now this desire is what the drunkard, the saint, the mystic hankers for in varying ways:—a purity, a final innocence—the phrase is Mr. Spender's. I think we Americans are very wistful about it. Yet we continue to make a fetish of "thing-hood," we surround ourselves with junk, ugly objects endlessly repeated in an economy dedicated to waste. Hence the possible relevance of my quotation from "Dolor," which I repeat in part:

> I have known the inexorable sadness of pencils,
> Neat in their boxes, dolor of pad and paper-weight, . . .
> And I have seen dust from the walls of institutions,
> Finer than flour, alive, more dangerous than silica,
> Sift, almost invisible, through long afternoons of tedium,
> Dropping a fine film on nails and delicate eyebrows,
> Glazing the pale hair, the duplicate gray standard faces.

This poem is an exposition of one of the modern hells: the institution that overwhelms the individual man. The "order," the trivia of the institution, is, in human terms, a disorder, and as such, must be resisted. It's truly a sign of psychic health that the young are already aware of this. How far-reaching all this is, how subtle its ramifications, how disastrous to the human psyche—to worship bigness, the firm, the university; numbers, even, let me say, the organized team effort.

The human problem is to find out what one really *is*: whether one exists, whether existence is possible. But how? "Am I but nothing, leaning toward a thing?" I think of what I wrote and felt nearly thirty years ago in a period of ill-health and economic terror—the first poem in my first book. The middle stanza says:

> My truths are all foreknown,
> This anguish self-revealed,
> I'm naked to the bone,
> With nakedness my shield.
> Myself is what I wear:
> I keep the spirit spare.

The last stanza was personally prophetic:

> *The anger will endure,*
> *The deed will speak the truth*
> *In language strict and pure.*
> *I stop the lying mouth:*
> *Rage warps my clearest cry*
> *To witless agony.*

All this has been said before, in Thoreau, in Rilke.

I was going through, though I didn't realize it at the time, a stage that all contemplative men must go through. This poem is a clumsy, innocent, desperate asseveration. I am not speaking of the empirical self, the flesh-bound ego; it's a single word: myself, the aggregate of the several selves, if you will. The spirit or soul—should we say the self, once perceived, becomes the soul?—this I was keeping "spare" in my desire for the essential. But the spirit need not be spare: it can grow gracefully and beautifully like a tendril, like a flower. I did not know this at the time. This sense I tried later to describe, metaphorically, many times:

> *The spirit moves,*
> *Yet stays:*
> *Stirs as a blossom stirs,*
> *Still wet from its bud-sheath,*
> *Slowly unfolding,*
> *Turning in the light with its tendrils;*
> *Plays as a minnow plays,*
> *Tethered to a limp weed, swinging,*
> *Tail around, nosing in and out of the current,*
> *Its shadows loose, a watery finger;*
> *Moves, like the snail,*
> *Still inward,*

> Taking and embracing its surroundings,
> Never wishing itself away,
> Unafraid of what it is,
> A music in a hood,
> A small thing,
> Singing.

Nor need this final self, or spirit, be a foulness, a disgusting thing from which we should be delivered. A stanza from Stanley Kunitz says:

> Father, the darkness of the self goes out
> And spreads contagion in the flowing air.
> I walk obscurely in a cloud of dark:
> Yea, when I kneeled, the dark kneeled down with me.
> Touch me: my folds and my defenses fall;
> I stand within myself, myself my shield.

This is far more complex than my little stanza, with a great line: "Yea, when I kneeled, the dark kneeled down with me." But this sense of contamination, the "my taste was me," is not a necessity: we need not be guilt-ridden— if we are pure in heart. It may, of course, as in the Kunitz stanza, be a prelude to a real psychic purgation.

But the young often do have an acute sense of defilement, a hatred of the body. Thus I remember marking this feeling in a violent little poem:

> I hate my epidermal dress,
> The savage blood's obscenity,
> The rags of my anatomy,
> And willingly would I dispense
> With false accouterments of sense,
> To sleep immodestly, a most
> Incarnadine and carnal ghost.

Hyperbole, of course, but behind it is still the same desire for a reality of the spirit. Again I was wrong. For the body should be cherished: a temple of God, some Christians say.*

In any quest for identity today—or any day—we run up inevitably against this problem: What to do with our ancestors? I mean it as an ambiguity: both the literal or blood, and the spiritual ancestors. Both, as we know, can overwhelm us. The devouring mother, the furious papa. And if we're trying to write, the Supreme Masters. In this same harried period, I wrote, in a not very good poem:

> Corruption reaps the young. You dread
> The menace of ancestral eyes
> Recoiling from the serpent head
> Of fate, you blubber in surprise. . . .

And so on . . . in the last stanza,

> You meditate upon the nerves,
> Inflame with hate. This ancient feud
> Is seldom won. The spirit starves
> Until the dead have been subdued.

I remember the late John Peale Bishop, that fine neglected poet, reading this and saying, "You're impassioned, but wrong. The dead can help us." And he was right; but it took me some years to learn that.

Let me say boldly, now, that the extent to which the great dead can be evoked, or can come to us, can be eerie, and astonishing. Let me, at the risk of seeming odd, recite a personal incident.

I was in that particular hell of the poet: a longish dry

* Roethke marked this paragraph "Omit" in his typescript.

period. It was 1952, I was 44, and I thought I was done. I was living alone in a biggish house in Edmonds, Washington. I had been reading—and re-reading—not Yeats, but Ralegh and Sir John Davies. I had been teaching the five-beat line for weeks—I knew quite a bit about it, but write it myself?—no: so I felt myself a fraud.

Suddenly, in the early evening, the poem "The Dance" started, and finished itself in a very short time—say thirty minutes, maybe in the greater part of an hour, it was all done. I felt, I *knew*, I had hit it. I walked around, and I wept; and I knelt down—I always do after I've written what I know is a good piece. But at the same time I had, as God is my witness, the actual sense of a Presence—as if Yeats himself were *in* that room. The experience was in a way terrifying, for it lasted at least half an hour. That house, I repeat, was charged with a psychic presence: the very walls seemed to shimmer. I wept for joy. At last I was somebody again. He, they—the poets dead—were with me.

Now I know there are any number of cynical explanations for this phenomenon: auto-suggestion, the unconscious playing an elaborate trick, and so on, but I accept none of them. It was one of the most profound experiences of my life.

If the dead can come to our aid in a quest for identity, so can the living—and I mean *all* living things, including the sub-human. This is not so much a naïve as a primitive attitude: animistic, maybe. Why not? Everything that lives is holy: I call upon these holy forms of life. One could even put this theologically: St. Thomas says, "God is above all things by the excellence of His nature; nevertheless, He is in all things as causing the being of all things." Therefore, in calling upon the snail, I am calling, in a sense, upon God:

> Snail, snail, glister me forward,
> Bird, soft-sigh me home.
> Worm, be with me.
> This is my hard time.

Or again, in a passage Mr. Bracken mentions:

> I could watch! I could watch!
> I saw the separateness of all things!
> My heart lifted up with the great grasses;
> The weeds believed me, and the nesting birds.

It is paradoxical that a very sharp sense of the being, the identity of some other being—and in some instances, even an inanimate thing—brings a corresponding heightening and awareness of one's own self, and, even more mysteriously, in some instances, a feeling of the oneness of the universe. Both feelings are not always present, I'm aware, but either can be an occasion for gratitude. And both can be induced. The first simply by intensity in the seeing. To look at a thing so long that you are a part of it and it is a part of you—Rilke gazing at his tiger for eight hours, for instance. If you can effect this, then you are by way of getting somewhere: knowing you will break from self-involvement, from I to Otherwise, or maybe even to Thee.

True, I'm speaking in these lines of a heightened consciousness. In the early part of that poem, nature was "dead," ambiguous, ominous. But the "angel," an emissary of the "other," was invoked; there was some kind of ritualistic, even penitential, act: "Was it dust I was kissing? . . . Alone, I kissed the skin of a stone."—the inanimate itself becomes alive before the final euphoria of this piece.

The second part of this feeling, the "oneness," is, of course, the first stage in mystical illumination, an experience many men have had, and still have: the sense that all is one and one is all. This is inevitably accompanied by a loss of the "I," the purely human ego, to another center, a sense of the absurdity of death, a return to a state of innocency.

This experience has come to me so many times, in so many varying circumstances, that I cannot suspect its validity: it is *not* one of the devil's traps, an hallucination, a voice, a snare. I can't claim that the soul, my soul, was absorbed in God. No, God for me still remains someone to be confronted, to be dueled with: that is perhaps my error, my sin of pride. But the oneness, Yes!

But let us return to the more homely but related form of exaltation: creativity itself. Can we say this: that the self can be found in love, in human, mutual love, in work that one loves—not in *arbeit* in the German sense? Think of what happened to them and is still happening. The novel, that secondary form, can teach us how to act; the poem, and music, how to feel: and the feeling is vastly more important. And the "creativity" may be vicarious. Once we feel deeply, to paraphrase Marianne Moore, we begin to behave.

And of all the instruments for verbal creativity close at hand today, the supreme example seems to me the short lyric.

When I was young, to make something in language, a poem that was all of a piece, a poem that could stand for what I was at the time—that seemed to be the most miraculous thing in the world. Most scholarship seemed irrelevant rubbish; most teachers seemed lacking in wisdom, in knowledge they had proved on their pulses. Certain writers called out to me: I believed them implicitly. I still do.

"We think by feeling. What is there to know?" This, in its essence, is a description of the metaphysical poet who thinks with his body: an idea for him can be as real as the smell of a flower or a blow on the head. And those so lucky as to bring their whole sensory equipment to bear on the process of thought grow faster, jump more frequently from one plateau to another more often.

And it is one of the ways man at least approaches the divine—in this comprehensive human act, the really good poem.

For there *is* a God, and He's here, immediate, accessible. I don't hold with those thinkers that believe in this time He is farther away—that in the Middle Ages, for instance, He was closer. He is equally accessible now, not only in works of art or in the glories of a particular religious service, or in the light, the aftermath that follows the dark night of the soul, but in the lowest forms of life, He moves and has His being. Nobody has killed off the snails. Is this a new thought? Hardly. But it needs some practicing in Western society. Could Reinhold Niebuhr love a worm? I doubt it. But I—we—can.

PART TWO

VERSE IN REHEARSAL

THERE ARE TIMES WHEN EVEN EXHIBITIONISM MAY SERVE a useful purpose. Let us hope this is one of the times, for I have been asked to show how verse may be revised and improved. This is a particularly dangerous business, because talking about poetry at any time is likely to be futile and vulgar. These verses have served me before, as part of a lecture in the verse writing course and in an appearance or two elsewhere. It is easy for me to be objective about them because they represent a phase of past experience.

My reasons originally for using this piece were several: I wanted to break down the reserves of the timid; I knew, as a teacher, that students are always more impressed by immediate, first-hand experience or knowledge, even though that experience or knowledge may not contain the whole truth; and finally because when I was seventeen and eighteen, I was desperately eager to see how particular work could be improved, to get the point of view of a practicing writer. In school we studied masterpieces; they were so good they discouraged me.

Here, then, is an example of bad verse slightly improved.

> This elemental force
> Was wrested from the sun;
> A river's leaping source
> Is locked in narrow bone.
>
> This love is lusty mirth
> That shakes eternal sky,
> The agony of birth,
> The fiercest will to die.
>
> The fever-heat of mind
> Within prehensile brute;
> A seed that swells the rind
> Of strange, impalpable fruit.
>
> This faith surviving shock,
> This smoldering desire,
> Will split its way through rock
> Like subterranean fire.

A letter from a friend, Rolfe Humphries, one of the editors of the old *Measure* and one of the best technicians among modern poets, explains the weaknesses of this draft far better than I could. I quote this with Mr. Humphries' permission, at the risk of raising the question whether my poems are not community or cooperative efforts.

32

About the poem you enclosed: possibly all I have to say is wide of the mark and not really about the poem at all. But I think of one or two sermon-ish remarks about technique, and will blame you for sending me the text and the impulse. The questions you wrote in hint your own doubts, the first two you can dismiss, and I'll try to meet the query of your third question— "fair traditional piece?" It is certainly in the historical and traditional manner but you could make more use of the manner, and exploit it to better advantage than you do here. If the editors have any intelligent reason for rejecting the poem, it may be that they are fighting shy of it on the ground of its conventional rhymes: desire-fire; shock-rock; mirth-birth; sky-die. It just misses breath-death, as it were; and is pretty trite, at least it must seem so to the conventional mind, almost regardless of where it is set. And personally I am a little bothered by your monogamous adjective-noun combinations: six such combinations in the first eight lines, while each may be used advisedly, is a good deal to ask the reader to endure; or, if he can achieve such endurance, you condition him to a frame of mind which he has to throw off with a most violent wrench when he comes to "strange, impalpable fruit." About that last phrase I do not know what to think, and wonder what you think yourself; my guess is either that you think it a mess or else consider it the central technical triumph of the poem. I am uncertain of its strength either as to sound or as to the adjective "strange," [which] by over-declaring, weakens the paradox, or saying "impalpable" in connection with fruit. If it is impalpable, that is strange enough. I think there is some other word, beginning with un-, a quadrisyllabic word that would eliminate "strange," or a trisyllabic one that would follow it. You have to go, metrically, too fast and bumpily with "impalpable" to get either the feeling of impalpable or strange. Is all this laboring the obvious? What I think could be done with this kind of poem is deliberately advertise the conventional by calling it "Poem with Old Rhymes" or something like that, and then work in the idea by way of counterpoint to the simplicity, and have it come out in the end, the emotion breaking the pattern as the faith the rock. Or another thing to do would be, in each of the first three stanzas, hold a rhyme in suspense and precipitate them all in the last stanza, viz.:

> This elemental force
> Descended from the sun
> Is locked in narrow bone—

This something or other else,—and so on, and keep the reader wondering what has happened to those rhymes until they clinch the poem at the end.

Mr. Humphries even made another re-arrangement of this first draft to illustrate his points. Unfortunately, I cannot locate this at present. My own final version,—nothing like his, I hasten to say,—which was finally printed in *The Nation*, follows:

GENESIS

> This elemental force
> Was wrested from the sun;
> A river's leaping source
> Is locked in narrow bone.
>
> This wisdom floods the mind,
> Invades quiescent blood;
> A seed that swells the rind
> To burst the fruit of good.
>
> A pearl within the brain,
> Secretion of the sense;
> Around a central grain
> A meaning grows immense.

The poem still has defects: a kind of grunt and groan rhythm, very boring to certain ears; metaphorical rock-jumping, also tiresome at times. The virtues, if any, must speak for themselves.

Of course these changes are only a crude representation of one stage in the making of a poem. A far better way to study this problem is to work with original manuscripts or facsimiles. But these are hard to get. Recognizing this difficulty, the library of the University of Buffalo has begun collecting early drafts of poems by modern writers and preserving them on micro-film. And a few writers are beginning to be less reticent about their processes of thought. For example Allen Tate in a recent *Virginia Quarterly Review* contributes a remarkable essay on the composition of one of his poems.

I have deliberately included the long excerpt from Mr. Humphries to pay my respects to a former mentor and to indicate how an older writer can help a younger. To some people it may seem brazen to enlist the advice of another in revising a poem. To me this attitude seems foolish. The poet's fidelity, as Stanley J. Kunitz has said, is to the poem. In my own case, many pieces are completed without asking for or accepting comment, but I have received valuable criticism, from time to time, from people ranging from practicing poets and editors to semi-literates who profess to hate poetry. The writer who maintains that he works without regard for the opinion of others is either a jackass or a pathological liar.

OPEN LETTER

Dear ——,

You must realize that only a most high regard for you as a person induces me to say anything. For don't most statements or credos degenerate into elaborate defenses of one's own sort of thing: into the sales talk, the odious pimping for oneself? And how vulgar to be solemn about miseries and agitations which one has been permitted to escape by the act of creation itself! Furthermore, these particular poems *—and I say this detachedly and humbly

* The poems following this introduction are: "The Lost Son," "The Shape of the Fire," "Child on Top of a Greenhouse," "Vernal Sentiment," "Academic," "My Papa's Waltz," "The Heron," "Interlude." Roethke seems, however, to be referring to the first two poems here.

—are not, in any final sense, mine at all: they are a piece of luck (good or bad, as you choose to judge). For once, in other words, I am an instrument.

But I can hear you saying, That's all very well, old fellow. An instrument, yes. But remember: a conscious instrument. It's no good your trying to play the blubbering boy or implying that you're some kind of over-size aeolian harp upon which strange winds play uncouth tunes. Or, you may continue, changing the metaphor, let's say you fish, patiently, in that dark pond, the unconscious, or dive in, with or without pants on, to come up festooned with dead cats, weeds, tin cans, and other fascinating debris— I still insist that my little request for a few more clues isn't the same as asking you to say hello mom on the television. There need be no undue exposure; you won't have to pontificate. Remember: some noble spirits in the past—Blake, Yeats, Rilke, and others—have been willing to hold forth on their own work. . . .

You see, dear————, I know your attitude so well that I find myself being caught up in it! But believe me: you will have no trouble if you approach these poems as a child would, naïvely, with your whole being awake, your faculties loose and alert. (A large order, I daresay!) Listen to them, for they are written to be heard, with the themes often coming alternately, as in music, and usually a partial resolution at the end. Each poem—there are now eight in all and there probably will be at least one more—is complete in itself; yet each in a sense is a stage in a kind of struggle out of the slime; part of a slow spiritual progress; an effort to be born, and later, to become something more. As an example, look at the development of one of the earliest of these, "The Lost Son":

It is the "easiest" of the longer ones, I think, because it follows a narrative line indicated by the titles of the first four sections: "The Flight," "The Pit," "The Gibber," "The Return." "The Flight" is just what it says it is: a terrified running away—with alternate periods of hallucinatory waiting (the voices, etc.); the protagonist so geared-up, so over-alive that he is hunting, like a primitive, for some animistic suggestion, some clue to existence from the sub-human. These he sees and yet does not see: they are almost tail-flicks, from another world, seen out of the corner of the eye. In a sense he goes in and out of rationality; he hangs in the balance between the human and the animal.

"The Pit" is a slowed-down section; a period of physical and psychic exhaustion. And other obsessions begin to appear (symbolized by mole, nest, fish). In "The Gibber" these obsessions begin to take hold; again there is a frenetic activity, then a lapsing back into almost a crooning serenity ("What a small song," etc.). The line, "Hath the rain a father?" is from Job—the only quotation in the piece. (A third of a line, notice—not a third of a poem.) The next rising agitation is rendered in terms of balked sexual experience, with an accompanying "rant," almost in the manner of the Elizabethans, and a subsequent near-blackout.

Section IV is a return, a return to a memory of childhood that comes back almost as in a dream, after the agitation and exhaustion of the earlier actions. The experience, again, is at once literal and symbolical. The "roses" are still breathing in the dark; and the fireman can pull them out, even from the fire. After the dark night, the morning brings with it the suggestion of a renewing light:

a coming of "Papa." Buried in the text are many little ambiguities, not all of which are absolutely essential to the central meaning of the poem. For instance, the "pipe-knock." With the coming of steam, the pipes begin knocking violently, in a greenhouse. But "Papa," or the florist, as he approached, often would knock the pipe he was smoking on the sides of the benches, or on the pipes. Then, with the coming of steam and "papa"—the papa on earth and heaven are blended—there is the sense of motion in the greenhouse, my symbol for the whole of life, a womb, a heaven-on-earth.

In the final untitled section, the illumination, the coming of light suggested at the end of the last passage occurs again, this time to the nearly-grown man. But the illumination is still only partly apprehended; he is still "waiting." The beginning of the next poem, "The Long Alley," is a relapse into sinuous river-imagery: an ambivalent brooding by the edge of the city. And then a new phase begins swiftly.

This crude account tells very little about what actually happens in the poem; but at least you can see that the method is cyclic. I believe that to go forward as a spiritual man it is necessary first to go back. Any history of the psyche (or allegorical journey) is bound to be a succession of experiences, similar yet dissimilar. There is a perpetual slipping-back, then a going-forward; but there is some "progress." Are not some experiences so powerful and so profound (I am not speaking of the merely compulsive) that they repeat themselves, thrust themselves upon us, again and again, with variation and change, each time bringing us closer to our own most particular (and thus most universal) reality? We go, as Yeats said, from exhaustion to exhaustion. To begin from the depths and come out—that is difficult; for few know where the depths are or can recognize them; or, if they do, are afraid.

Some of these pieces, then, begin in the mire; as if man is no more than a shape writhing from the old rock. This may be due, in part, to the Michigan from which I come. Sometimes one gets the feeling that not even the animals have been there before; but the marsh, the mire, the Void, is always there, immediate and terrifying. It is a splendid place for schooling the spirit. It is America.

None the less, in spite of all the muck and welter, the dark, the *dreck* of these poems, I count myself among the happy poets. "I proclaim, once more, a condition of joy!" says the very last piece. All cats and agitations are not the same in the dark; likewise, each ecstasy has, I think, its special character. For instance in a later piece, "Praise to the End!" a particular (erotic) act occurs, then is accounted for by nonsense songs out of the past. There are laments for lost powers and then a euphoric passage, a sublimation of the original impulse in an ecstasy; but—and this is the point—in this passage the protagonist, for all his joy, is still "alone," and only one line mentions anything human:

"I've crawled from the mire, alert as a saint or a dog." Except for the saint, everything else is dog, fish, minnow, bird, etc., and the euphoric ride resolves itself into a death-wish. Equationally, the poem can be represented: onanism equals death, and even the early testament moralists can march out happily. (Is the protagonist "happy" in his death-wish? Is he a mindless euphoric jigger who goes blithering into oblivion? No. In terms of the whole sequence, he survives: this is a dead-end explored. His self-consciousness, his very will to live saves him from the annihilation of the ecstasy.)

Each of these poems presented its own series of problems. The earliest piece of all (in terms of the age of the protagonist) is written entirely from the viewpoint of a very small child: all interior drama; no comment; no interpretation. To keep the rhythms, the language "right," i.e. consistent with what a child would say or at least to create the "as if" of the child's world, was very difficult technically. I don't believe anyone else has been foolish enough to attempt a tragedy in this particular way. The rhythms are very slow; there is no cutesy prattle; it is not a suite in goo-goo.

A word or two about habits of mind or technical effects peculiar to this sequence. ("Peculiar" is not used in the sense of odd, for they are traditional poems. Their ancestors: German and English folk literature, particularly Mother Goose; Elizabethan and Jacobean drama, especially the songs and rants; the Bible; Blake and Traherne; Dürer.) Much of the action is implied or, particularly in the case of erotic experience, rendered obliquely. The revelation of the identity of the speaker may itself be a part of the drama; or, in some instances, in a dream sequence, his identity may merge with someone else's, or be deliberately blurred. This struggle for spiritual identity is, of course, one of the perpetual recurrences. (This is not the same as the fight of the adolescent personality for recognition in the "real" world.) Disassociation often precedes a new state of clarity.

Rhythmically, it's the spring and rush of the child I'm after—and Gammer Gurton's concision: *mütterkin's* wisdom. Most of the time the material seems to demand a

varied short line. I believe that, in this kind of poem, the
poet, in order to be true to what is most universal in him-
self, should not rely on allusion; should not comment or
employ many judgment words; should not meditate (or
maunder). He must scorn being "mysterious" or loosely
oracular, but be willing to face up to genuine mystery.
His language must be compelling and immediate: he must
create an actuality. He must be able to telescope image
and symbol, if necessary, without relying on the obvious
connectives: to speak in a kind of psychic shorthand when
his protagonist is under great stress. He must be able to
shift his rhythms rapidly, the "tension." He works intui-
tively, and the final form of his poem must be imagina-
tively right. If intensity has compressed the language so
it seems, on early reading, obscure, this obscurity should
break open suddenly for the serious reader who can hear
the language: the "meaning" itself should come as a dra-
matic revelation, an excitement. The clues will be scat-
tered richly—as life scatters them; the symbols will mean
what they usually mean—and sometimes something more.

Perhaps I have made these remarks sound like stric-
tures; if so, the phrase "in this kind of poem" should
precede each one. I don't mean to imply that these poems
fulfill such rigorous requirements or that their substance
or their technique represents an answer to anything, a
"direction." It is a dark world in which to work and the
demands, other than technical, made upon the writer are
savage. Even these words come painfully—and I doubt
that they have much value. I remember a statement from
Jung that turned up in a student's notebook. "The truth
is that poets are human beings, and that what a poet has

to say about his work is far from being the most illuminating word on the subject."

So, *kind*, throw all this away and read them aloud!

Love,

T.

The next phase? Something much longer: dramatic and *playable*. Pray for me.

THE TEACHING POET

I AM QUITE WILLING TO ABIDE BY THE EVIDENCE—THE WORK done—although if it were rubbish I still believe the effort justified. The lyric, particularly the short lyric, is a great teaching instrument. It's all there, all of a piece, a comprehensive act. Even to "hear" a good poem carries us far beyond the ordinary in education. And to write a verse, or even a piece of verse, however awkward and crude, that bears some mark, something characteristic of the author's true nature—that is, I insist, a considerable human achievement.

Let's say no one would claim to make poets. But a good deal can be taught about the craft of verse. A few people come together, establish an intellectual and emotional climate wherein creation is possible. They teach each other—that ideal condition of what once was called "progressive education." They learn by doing. Something of the creative lost in childhood is recovered. The student (and teacher) learn a considerable something about themselves and the language. The making of verse remains a human activity.

There's no point in being grandiose about results. How many in any one generation are true poets? Some may be in a class just to improve their prose—and that's all right. Some may be there to get a further insight into what a poem is. Undoubtedly some of them write because they are young. They may be mixed up, and the poem for them is a way out—yet something more than a psychological excrescence. It should be listened to and, in many instances, honored. I can't share the disdain many professionals have for the serious amateur.

It's a departure, verse writing is, from the ordinary run of things in a college—for almost all thinking has been directed toward analysis, a breaking-down, whereas the metaphor is a synthesis, a building-up, a creation of a new world, however incomplete, crude, tawdry, naïve it may be. It will have, for better or worse, its own shape and form and identity—and how often can that be said of thinking today?

The class in writing poetry is a collective, cooperative act—most of the time. But to bring diverse people, including the neurotic, the pig-headed, the badly trained, into harmony is a task that must be assumed, at first, by the teacher and carried on without the appearance of a struggle. One compulsive, one older person who has been overpraised by the vanity presses, can make everybody freeze up. Discussions have to be free and easy, otherwise the whole method breaks down. And often, during the first weeks, the instructor has to bring all his energy, tact, teaching wisdom into play in order to get a genuine rapport, a sense of mutual respect.

Sometimes it is best to let matters develop from work at hand: old poems or new. In presenting these, the author provides enough carbons for everyone to see the piece on the page. He reads it, and some other voice reads it. Often, in the case of embarrassingly weak work, it's best to ask firmly for positive reactions first.

Some have difficulty verbalizing about the aesthetic experience. But often their gropings make for the fresh insight. There is little shadow-boxing with terminology. The problem is to seize upon what is worth preserving in immature work—the single phrase of real poetry, the line that has energy—and to build it into a complete piece that has its own shape and motion. To this task students bring their candor, their explicitness, and, often, their truly fresh and naïve ears. The great lesson of cutting comes up again and again, but the applications are various. The war on the cliché is continuous, but poetry is not written by mere avoidance of the cliché. Little theorizing about rhythm, but a constant reading aloud to hear rhythms, to get a notion of how language flows. Essentially this is teaching by ear, by suggestion, by insinuation. Cross-references are thrown out repeatedly, and sometimes received and assimilated: a rain of examples, often from obscure or minor sources. Why? Either to imitate consciously or to look at and do otherwise. I use a great body of mimeographed material and several anthologies and collected editions; and the University has built special cases in the classroom so I can run to my own books in pursuing this referential technique. There is a constant effort to remind students that poetry is a classic art and requires that its exponents read intensively in all literatures.

Each student is expected to revise pieces when necessary and to preserve successive versions in a workbook handed in at the end of the course. He also includes the results of his reading in a selective anthology of his own making—somewhat on the order of Edith Sitwell's *Notebooks*—consisting of remarks on craft, good lines, poems, anything that has been genuinely pertinent to his development. This is not a mere scrapbook or piece of intellectual window-dressing, but a highly personal compilation, often showing that the anthology can be a creative act.

There are several possible points of departure in group assignments: to play with sound; to work with a particular stanza form; to begin with strongly stressed simple poems, such as nursery rhymes. This last is hardest but probably best if the group is young and unspoiled.

The scheme is that every student pursue his own bent, write the poems he wants to write—and also do at least some set exercises as a discipline. The discipline may lie in composing a poem without adjectives; a poem based on adjectives—or perhaps sets of verbs, nouns, and adjectives; a straight observational piece, with or without analogy; a poem based on a single figure; a revision of someone else's bad poem (Braithwaite and Moult are rich mines of examples); a translation; a poem developed from a first line; a poem of which first and third stanzas are provided; a song (some make a setting, too); a poem involving an incident; a piece of original rhythmical prose—and later a poem evolved from it; a dialogue in verse; a "hate" poem; or a letter in verse.

"Form" is thought of as a sieve, to use Auden's metaphor, for catching certain kinds of material. Even a shabby pattern like the tetrameter couplet will throw the student back on the language and force him to be conscious of words as a medium; also it will teach him how to shape the sentence to a particular end, to get effects with full and off-rhyme, and to manage the polysyllable. He can embrace the form or resist it—either result can be useful.

Every teacher has certain gimmicks, stunts, favorite examples which he knows will work—often because he cares about them and brings to them an enthusiasm that carries conviction. For instance, in discussing a form, to quote a poem from memory while walking around the room, then to write it on the board, carrying on an analysis as I write is more effective, usually, than just turning to what's in a book, even though I use beautiful texts like Bullett's *The English Galaxy* or *The Collected Poems of W. B. Yeats*. But it is possible for a course dealing with what really matters to complicated people to become, like New York, too stimulating. I remember a class on the epigram—everybody got into the act: we had a wonderful time quoting ribald snatches from the Elizabethans, Jonson, Prior; the more uninhibited Irish. And there was, I think, some pertinent advice. It was a "good" class; however, the "epigrams" that came in later were abominable. Why? Perhaps our euphoria had left us addled. Perhaps the epigram is a form that lends itself only to maturity, to a special sort of embittered wisdom that life brings later.

The perfect example. How we academics hunt and cherish it! One that won't scare the slowest, that is within the ken of the earnest apprentice, and yet won't bore the most gifted in the class. I use, to exemplify the tetrameter couplet, a poem like Stanley Kunitz's "Change," not his best piece, but one with structural devices, a technical cunning that can be made immediately apparent to listeners. It is excellent for such obvious things as its introductory participial phrase, the modifier before and after the noun, the absolute construction, the tercet—as well as subtleties in rhythm and meaning. Another example is Herrick's "A Sweet Disorder," with its wonderfully managed epithets and light rhymes, its levels of meaning in the apparently artless verse. Still another is Marvell's "To His Coy Mistress"; in fact, almost anything he did in the form can be used. Or consider Vaughan. Or Charles Cotton. Or Cowley's "The thirsty earth" in its superb plain style. But suppose some co-ed cries, "I want to write lyrics! This form is for wit-writing." The answer might be a blast of Bogan's "The Alchemist," where the simple declarative sentences make for powerful effects. Then from there the class might move on to Bridges and Campion and Jonson.

At its highest level this kind of class might become like the poem itself, in that the full powers of the associational forces of the mind (or, rather, not one mind, but several) are brought into play. (The simile comes from a student, Mr. Claire J. Fox.) I'm not aware of ever initiating any such dance of the mind and heart, but I have seen collective excitement in a class rise to a point where even slips of the tongue or misunderstandings provided a further insight. "He should anchor the abstraction." "That's it—to anger the abstraction"—a metaphor for me evocative and profound.

To be sure, teaching is not the communication, or even

intercommunication, of excitement. The test, obviously, is whether the ultimate result is healthy-mindedness, is good work. But again you can't tell. Often, in teaching, the payoff is far in the future.

There are those who say the young have nothing to write about. This is wrong. For one thing there is the whole world of adolescence which they are in or have just departed from, with all its vagaries, its ambiguous loyalties, its special poignance. There are memories of childhood, still vivid in many instances. And they can go outside and look at things with a fresh eye.

My own shortcomings in this kind of course are many. I doubt whether I insist enough on technical finish, as, say, Winters or Humphries or Ransom might. I am perhaps unduly rough on the student who wants a mentor, a Papa. You can't go out all the way; you can't carry their spiritual burdens. I insist that the teaching poet preserve his identity; otherwise he may not only ruin his own writing and thereby lose his effectiveness with the best students, but he will also do them another disservice: unconsciously he will begin trying to create them in his own image.

The conference has its place, but most knowledge of technique is acquired obliquely. One suggestion, one lead, after class or in the hall, if really the thing needful at that particular time, is worth far more than any number of pipe-sucking, pencil-poking, lugubrious sessions in the office.

The surprises are in psychological growth. As in piano-playing, suddenly, for no explicable reason, someone jumps to an entirely different plateau of performance and understanding. A boy who has memorized most of Eddie

Guest will appear with a poem, rough maybe, but a real "splinter of feeling."

Most teaching is visceral, and the genial uproar that constitutes a verse class, especially so. It is as ephemeral as the dance, and as hard to localize or define. It is what is left after all the reading and thinking and reciting: the residue, the illumination.

A WORD TO THE INSTRUCTOR

I SHOULD LIKE TO GIVE, HUMBLY AND SIMPLY, SOME GEN-eral advice on the teaching of poetry, based on my own mistakes and shortcomings. I assume a young instructor, in a place strange to him, faced with a mixed section of students, frightened as I am still frightened after thirty-five years' experience, before a first class.

What, then, to do? I remind myself I must

1. Establish a rapport, get a sense of communication with the whole class—and quickly. This means breaking right into the heart of things at the start: making the students aware of poetry as experience, making them hear it. It means keeping as many antennae out as pos-

sible, keeping oneself "open," aware of everyone, not just the two or three best. It means hard work: keeping on a full steam of psychic energy from the very beginning—or every day becomes Monday morning. It's wiser to begin with material you know like the back of your hand, rather than start off by generalities about poetry, or by a learned preamble of historical background. Ideally, the instructor should have the voice, the physical presence to present the poem for what it is. Not all of us are born with the voice box of Dylan Thomas or Siobhan McKenna. But if a teacher cares about what he is up to, carries the conviction that poetry is the supreme art, in language at least; that poetry, even of the second or third order represents a fast way into wisdom, to the insights of the race—he will not have trouble bringing even the most diverse class, including the lumpish and the earless, along with him. True, most of us, from time to time, should do some candid auditory testing: find out (preferably before a pair of critical ears) what we really sound like, and even do a bit of rehearsing. The ideal classroom voice for poetry, of course, should not be heavily dramatic or too carefully articulated, but detached, maybe a little "dry" even, so the poem can be rendered exactly, without the intrusion of personality. I think of I. A. Richards, in 1931 at Harvard, reading, say, Bridges or De la Mare, as the closest thing to perfection, in this respect, I have ever heard. Some poems do require "blasting," Donne or Browning, for instance, and Crazy Jane needs her special vehemence. But we must remember not to equate noise with passion. And if your voice is on the thin or reedy side, rely more on records—or let the students themselves, particularly later in the course, do some of the reading. This need not mean, God forbid, turning the class into "oral interpretation." Yet often, when pressed for time, throwing a shy one half-a-dozen lines will tell you much about a student, will do wonders in breaking down inhibitions, particularly if you type-cast a bit: give the student what he can handle. You may find a dolt in discussion with a voice, real rhythmical sense.

2. Wear learning as lightly and easily as possible. It's healthier at the very start to make plain that you don't know all there's to know about the poems under discussion or their authors—and don't pretend to: then you can operate openly and candidly, elucidate with grace and precision, rather than guardedly and arthritically, with all the academic whereto's and why's. I remember Robert Frost saying in conversation, "Let's be accurate, but not too accurate"—the viewpoint of the writer, not the scholar, I daresay. But certainly the notion that teacher is omniscient, or ought to be, should be dispelled immediately and promptly. Sometimes it's hard for a young man, fresh from his Ph.D. orals, to believe this. Nudge him with a name or a poem, and he starts spilling information, often irrelevant. And there are other traps the learned young can fall into: approaching material on the knees (Poundlings and followers of Eliot are particularly prone to this), riding a particular thesis (Freudians, Jungians, devotees of Papa Kenneth Burke often offend in this respect), or aping the attitudes or mannerisms of some previous teacher, and so on.

But to return to more positive matters:

3. Vary the pace, the attack, the methods of approach. This is of vast importance, and can be easily forgotten. Since, as any competent young teacher quickly learns, every lecture or discussion section, whether of freshmen or graduate students, varies from year to year, from quarter to quarter, the possibilities here are endless. To respect the individual student's viewpoint, to carry in the mind, whether one wants to or not, what a particular student has said or written, to come back to his idea or attitude at the right time—if it deserves coming back to—this I find the most exhausting aspect of teaching. It is also the point of greatest danger both to instructor and student. For the fanatical teacher can overwhelm the impressionable, and he likewise can become too involved in the attitudes, the psyches of the young to the point of his own self-destruction. Thus, more than memory or mere audience sense is involved, and even the young teacher must keep his distance, his dignity, and be content with a limited, a human effort. It's well to remember that even the most fervent can't endure intense lyric poetry all the time; that a class can be a dance, but a course is not a dance marathon; that even freshmen can become hideously expert at text-creeping. Some poems need, demand, a careful exegesis, obviously; others simply should be read and enjoyed, perhaps with a few swift comments, or with no comment at all. And sometimes even the most relaxed, rambling, apparently irrelevant session may open up more than a turgid recital or display of learning. The aside, trivial or rich, or even the gag, unstrained—is often the very thing, alas, as every teacher knows, that will be remembered; in fact, there's

a type of student that seems to wait for just the "good-ies," the nuggets that crop up from the unconscious. But take my word for it, the canned joke, the studied effect, is usually fatal, particularly for the teacher only a few years older than his class. They may laugh, po-litely; or they may freeze on you, and then it can get very lonely, behind or in front of the desk, the podium.

One last word. This anthology, uncluttered with opin-ions and apparatus, will come to certain students at the very climax of their reading years—seventeen and eighteen —when the hunger for the best is often acute, yet vague, unchannelled, or already partly debased by rubbish. No text, no anthology, can be the answer to everything. But *Twelve Poets*—I can say this because I have had nothing to do with the choices—embodies, I am convinced, real teaching wisdom. There is enough here to engage the brightest: to give any young person a sense of what tradi-tion is in the English language. It can stand being em-braced, or resisted. I only wish that, in September 1925, someone had thrust such a book upon me. And saw to it that I read it closely, and knew slugs of it by heart.

THEODORE ROETHKE
WRITES . . .

IT IS AN ESPECIAL PLEASURE FOR AN AMERICAN TO THANK the Poetry Book Society for making *Words for the Wind* its Christmas choice.

The volume really consists of two books: earlier work and later. Since it is his last things which most interest a poet, let me dwell on these briefly.

I believe a book should reveal as many sides of a writer as is decent for him to show: that these aspects be brought together in some kind of coherent whole that is recognizable to the careful reader. This means that some poems will sometimes support other poems, either by being complements to them, or by providing contrasts. Thus, the first section of love poems in Words for the Wind contains pieces tender or highly romantic, others are "witty," coarse and sensual. It is my hope that a reader will like both kinds of thing. Then by way of contrast, there is a handful of light pieces and poems for children. These are rougher than what most children's editors prefer. The attempt—part of a larger effort—was to make poems which please both child and parent, without insulting the intelligence or taste of either.

The third section of these later pieces consists of poems of terror, and running away—and the dissociation of personality that occurs in such attempts to escape reality. In these the protagonist is alive in space, almost against his will; his world is the cold and dark known to sub-human things.

There follows a series of poems dedicated to W. B. Yeats. Highly formal stylistically, these poems are related to the sixteenth century, with lines severely end-stopped, for the most part.

Finally comes a sequence of longish poems "Meditations of an Old Woman." The protagonist is modelled, in part, after my own mother, now dead, whose favorite reading was the Bible, Jane Austen, and Dostoyevsky—in other words, a gentle, highly articulate old lady believing in the glories of the world, yet fully conscious of its evils. These poems use a technique of developing themes alternately, a method employed in "Praise to the End!," an earlier sequence, a kind of spiritual autobiography beginning with the very small child. Of these last poems I have said: *

. . . Much of the action is implied or, particularly in the case of erotic experience, rendered obliquely. The revelation of the identity of the speaker may itself be a part of the drama; or, in some instances, in a dream sequence, his identity may merge with someone else's, or be deliberately blurred. This struggle for spiritual identity is, of course, one of the perpetual recurrences. (This is not the same as the fight of the adolescent personality for recognition in the "real" world.) Disassociation often precedes a new state of clarity.

Rhythmically, it's the spring and rush of the child I'm after—and Gammer Gurton's concision: *mütterkin's* wisdom. Most of the time the material seems to demand a varied short line. I believe that, in this kind of poem, the poet, in order to be true to what is most universal in himself, should not rely on allusion; should not comment or employ many judgment words; should not meditate (or maunder). He must scorn being "mysterious" or loosely oracular, but be willing to face up to genuine mystery. His language must be compelling and immediate: he must create an actuality. He must be able to telescope image and symbol, if necessary, without relying on the obvious connectives: to speak in a kind of psychic shorthand when his protagonist is under great stress. He must be able to shift his rhythms rapidly, the "tension." He works intuitively, and the final form of the poem must be imaginatively right. If intensity has compressed the language so it seems, on early reading, obscure, this obscurity should break open suddenly for the serious reader who can hear the language: the "meaning" itself should come as a dramatic revelation, an excitement. The clues will be scattered richly—as life scatters them; the symbols will mean what they usually mean—and sometimes something more.

* In "Open Letter," from *Mid-Century American Poets*, edited by John Ciardi. The full text of "Open Letter" is given in the present collection.

Words for the Wind opens with some very plain little bits of verse and descriptive pieces about a greenhouse I grew up in and around.

But it is the longish pieces that really break the ground —if any ground is broken. And it is these that I hope the younger readers, in particular, will come to cherish.

I think of myself as a poet of love, a poet of praise. And I wish to be read aloud.

HOW TO WRITE LIKE
SOMEBODY ELSE

A GOOD DEAL OF NONSENSE HAS BEEN WRITTEN ABOUT "IN-fluence" in modern poetry, particularly the influence of one contemporary by another—by writers not very secure in their own practice who would have us believe that even their laundry notes are the result of divine visitation; by reviewers of limited taste and sensibility; by anthologists; and by the glib and middle-aging young who sometimes debase the role of *enfant terrible* by applying to the practice of criticism the methods—and often the taste—of the radio gagman.

For them it's all quite simple: any alliteration, any compounding, any enthusiasm before nature equals Hopkins; any concern with man in society or the use of two "definite" articles in a row is "Audenesque"; any associational shifting or developing a theme alternately, as in music, is Eliot; sexual imagery or a dense language structure, Thomas; and so on.

A little humility may be in order. Let us say that some people—often inarticulate simple types—can hear a poem, can recognize the real thing; far fewer know what a line is; and fewer yet, I suspect, are equipped to determine finally whether a writer has achieved his own tone, or whether he has been unduly influenced by another; for such a judgment involves a truly intimate knowledge not only of the particular writers concerned, but also the whole tradition of the language; a very exact medium sense; and a delicate and perceptive ear. I suggest that the central critical problem remains: whether a real poem has been created. If it has, the matter of influence becomes irrelevant. Think of the sons of Ben; think of Herbert. Is he any less a poet because he took over some of Donne's effects? Is Auden a charlatan because he read and profited by reading Owen, Laura Riding, Robert Graves?

In a shrewd justification of the referential poem, or less charitably, the poem which is an anthology of other men's effects, Eliot said, "Bad poets imitate; good poets steal." In other words, take what you will with authority and see that you give it another, or even better life, in the new context.

All true, but in some ways a terrifying remark for the beginning writer, who is often neither bad nor good, but simply, as yet, unformed. He isn't sure whether he is a thief or a fake. He may, critically, be far ahead of himself emotionally. He may be able to discuss, with real intelligence, Marvell or Pound or Stevens, but when he takes pen in hand the great models of the past may seem far away and even absurd, and the big names of his own time awesome, overwhelming. Particularly if he is a provincial far from a good library, or from any practicing poet, the immediately preceding literary generation, or the more precocious around his own age—and not always the best of these—may exercise a powerful attraction. The sensitive young are always acutely conscious of "fashion," highly aware of the topical, the surfaces of life; there is a peculiar sheen of contemporaneousness—the phrase may be Huxley's—which seems to exist to speak to them alone. They may be attracted by those writers who reflect their own confusions: the roaring-ass "primitive" produced on both sides of the Atlantic; or they can turn to the overneat technicians who simplify experience by forcing it into an arbitrary order.

To such a young man in such a state I introduce the following examples, my own transgressions, in the hope he will take heart and do otherwise:

This Light

This light is the very flush of spring; it is innocent and warm;
It is gentle as celestial rain; it is mellow as gold;
Its pure effulgence may unbind the form
Of a blossoming tree; it may quicken fallow mould.

This light is various and strange; its luminous hue
May transmute the bleakest dust to silver snow;
Its radiance may be caught within a pool, a bead of dew;
It may contract to the sheerest point; it may arch to a bow.

*This light is heaven's transcendent boon, a beam
Of infinite calm; it will never cease;
It will illuminate forever the aether-stream;
This light will lead me to eventual peace.*

This example illustrates, certainly, at least two things: a wrong choice of diction; an unfortunate use of a model. The model is Elinor Wylie; the moral is: don't imitate an imitator; pastiche begets pastiche.

One of the great and early temptations is Beautiful Words. How they shimmer, those mellifluous counters that others have used so often. It's the stage Yeats was at when he murmured, "Words alone are certain good," against which can be set Hopkins' "Words alone are only words." But even Hopkins cared for "lovely" for instance.

Now I didn't clutch a copy of Wylie in one hand, and write the piece with the other. Actually, I had been reading a lot of Vaughan, and a friend of mine suggested I do a poem on "Light." I took—I suppose from Wylie—the devices of metaphor on a string—as in her piece

*This sorrow was small and vulnerable and shortlived;
It was neither earth nor stone . . .*

which itself derives, I believe, from Shelley.

To adopt the technical device was legitimate: my real blunder was not to make the poem better: it's static; it doesn't develop; the epithets have too much to do; the last line is a banality.

My next spiritual romance was with Léonie Adams—something else again: her rhythms far subtler and more varied, a much richer aura of suggestiveness.

Listen to this:

The Buds Now Stretch

The buds now stretch into the light,
The warm air stirs the fertile bough,
The sap runs free, and in the night
The young emergent leaf is cast;
The leaf is cast, and garish now,
And drunk with mellow gold, the green
Shapes to the accurate wind, though fast
Upon the branch are laggard leaves,
Their shade not finger-dies, but soon
Their patterns swing into the light
And broaden in the blaze of noon.
The substance of the tree is hung,
And all its loveliness unbound,
Its emerald leaves to sky are flung;
But that sweet vertical, the sun,
Repeats those leaves upon the ground
To deepen half a summer field.
And still as dreams that lovely yield
Of shadows bound like garnered sheaves,
A harvest of immobile shade:
But when those shadows move, a sound,
The full and level noise of leaves.

It's the Adams cadence, the hurrying of syllables into speech, as in:

It was my life, or so I said,
And I did well, forsaking it,
To go as quickly as the dead.

The technical trick is in the manipulation of the pause, the caesura, on the fourth and sixth syllables. But, alas, there are verbal, as well as rhythmical echoes: in "Kennst du das Land," this Adams has a line

> *Knew the leaves deepening the green ground.*

While I say

> *To deepen half a summer field.*

Maybe that's not so reprehensible; but she also says, elsewhere,

> *As sweet as bones which stretch from sleep,*

and in "Country Summer":

> *And full and golden is the yield*

and I say

> *As still as dreams that lovely yield*
> *Of shadows bound like garnered sheaves.*

I hate to abandon that poem: I feel it's something Miss Adams and I have created: a literary lovechild. Put it this way: I loved her so much, her poetry, that I just *had* to become, for a brief moment, a part of her world. For it *is* her world, and I had filled myself with it, and I *had* to create something that would honor her in her own terms. That, I think, expresses as best I can what really goes on with the hero- or heroine-worshiping young. I didn't cabbage those effects in cold blood; that poem is a true release in its way. I was too clumsy and stupid to articulate my own emotions: she helped me to say something about the external world, helped me convince myself that maybe, if I kept at it, eventually I might write a poem of my own, with the accent on my own speech.

Thus, one can stake out an area of subject matter, hoard up a body of words, even embody fresh observation in a sustained rhythm, in a poem all of a piece, and *still* be too close to somebody else. I limit myself to passages:

Diffuse the outpourings of the spiritual coward,
The rambling lies invented for the sick.
O see the fate of him whose guard was lowered!—
A single misstep and we leave the quick.

or

The winds of hatred blow
Cold, cold across the flesh
And chill the anxious heart,
Intricate phobias grow
From each malignant wish
To spoil collective life.
Now each man stands apart.

That, of course, is Wystan Hugh Auden, himself a real
magpie, with a cormorant's rapacity and the long mem-
ory of the elephant. He pillages the past, as in

"O where are you going?" said reader to rider,

from "The Cutty Wren":

"Oh where are you going?" says Milder to Malder

Or the present; here is Graves' "Full Moon":

As I walked out that sultry night,
I heard the stroke of One.
The moon, attained to her full height,
Stood beaming like the sun:
She exorcized the ghostly wheat
To mute assent in love's defeat,
Whose tryst had now begun.
The fields lay sick beneath my tread.

And Auden himself opens up a ballad:

> As I walked out one evening,
>   Walking down Bristol Street,
> The crowds upon the pavement
>   Were fields of harvest wheat.

And writes an entirely different poem. Now whether his conscious or unconscious mind seized on these elements: the "As I walked out," the street, the wheat, the fields, makes no difference. And it's perfectly possible that he might never have seen Graves' poem, or even written his earlier. But Auden, when he does take over a technical device or even another attitude, for the moment, does so with assurance and style. Invariably the poem moves into its own life.

Is this ever the case in my own practice? Well, I offer this as, possibly, an influence survived:

THE DANCE

> Is that dance slowing in the mind of man
> That made him think the universe could hum?
> The great wheel turns its axle when it can;
> I need a place to sing, and dancing-room,
> And I have made a promise to my ears
> I'll sing and whistle romping with the bears.
>
> For they are all my friends: I saw one slide
> Down a steep hillside on a cake of ice,—
> Or was that in a book? I think with pride:
> A caged bear rarely does the same thing twice
> In the same way: O watch his body sway!—
> This animal remembering to be gay.
>
> I tried to fling my shadow at the moon,
> The while my blood leaped with a wordless song.
> Though dancing needs a master, I had none

To teach my toes to listen to my tongue.
But what I learned there, dancing all alone,
Was not the joyless motion of a stone.

I take this cadence from a man named Yeats;
I take it, and I give it back again:
For other tunes and other wanton beats
Have tossed my heart and fiddled through my brain.
Yes, I was dancing-mad, and how
That came to be the bears and Yeats would know.

Oddly enough, the line "I take this cadence, etc." is, in a sense, a fib. I had been reading deeply in Ralegh, and in Sir John Davies; and they rather than Willie are the true ghosts in that piece.

Is it an effrontery to summarize? Imitation, conscious imitation, is one of the great methods, perhaps *the* method of learning to write. The ancients, the Elizabethans, knew this, profited by it, and were not disturbed. As a son of Ben, Herrick more than once rewrote Jonson, who, in turn, drew heavily on the classics. And so on. The poems are not less good for this: the final triumph is what the language does, not what the poet can do, or display. The poet's ultimate loyalty—the phrase belongs to Stanley Kunitz—is to the poem. The language itself is a compound, or, to change the figure, a bitch. The paradoxical thing, as R. P. Blackmur said of some of the young in the 'thirties, is that the most original poets are the most imitative. The remark is profound: if a writer has something to say, it will come through. The very fact he has the support of a tradition, or an older writer, will enable him to be more himself—or more than himself.

In a time when the romantic notion of the inspired

poet still has considerable credence, true "imitation" takes a certain courage. One dares to stand up to a great style, to compete with papa. In my own case, I should like to think I have over-acknowledged, in one way and another, my debt to Yeats. One simple device provides, I believe, an important technical difference: in the pentameter, I end-stop almost every line—a thing more usual when the resources of the language were more limited. This is not necessarily a virtue—indeed, from many points of view, a limitation. But it is part of an effort, however clumsy, to bring the language back to bare, hard, even terrible statement. All this Yeats himself, a bowerbird if there ever was one, would have understood, and, possibly, approved.

SOME REMARKS ON RHYTHM

What do *I* like? Listen:

> *Hinx, minx, the old witch winks!*
> *The fat begins to fry!*
> *There's nobody home but Jumping Joan,*
> *And father, and mother, and I.*

Now what makes that "catchy," to use Mr. Frost's word?
For one thing: the rhythm. Five stresses out of a possible
six in the first line, though maybe "old" doesn't take quite
as strong a stress as the others. And three—keep noticing
that magic number—internal rhymes, *hinx, minx, winks.*
And notice too the apparent mysteriousness of the action:
something happens right away—the old witch winks and
she sets events into motion. The fat begins to fry, liter-

ally and symbolically. She commands—no old fool witch this one. Notice that the second line, "The fat begins to fry," is absolutely regular metrically. It's all iambs, a thing that often occurs when previous lines are sprung or heavily counterpointed. The author doesn't want to get too far from his base, from his ground beat. The third line varies again with an anapaest and variations in the "o" and "u" sounds. "There's nobody home but Jumping Joan." Then the last line—anapaest lengthening the line out to satisfy the ear, "And father, and mother, and I." Sometimes we are inclined to feel that Mother Goose, or the traditional kind of thing, is almost infallible as memorable speech— the phrase is Auden's. But this is by no means so. There is another version that goes,

> Hink, mink, the old witch stinks,
> The fat begins to fry:
> Nobody's home but Jumping Joan,
> Jumping Joan and I.

Well, the whole situation has obviously altered, for the better perhaps from the standpoint of the speaker at least. But in his excitement he has produced a much inferior poem.

First, deleting the "x" 's takes some of the force away from the three rhyming words—"Hinx, minx, the old witch winks,"—the triad. What's more, he has become tiresomely naturalistic. "The old witch stinks"—hardly a fresh piece of observation. *Stinks* is a splendid old word, but here it is a bore. It is a prerogative of old witches to stink: part of their stock in trade as it were, and nobody mentions it. Take the change from *minx*, which means of course a pert little vixen of a girl, and carries with it overtones of tenderness; or, further back, a wanton, a roaring girl. And the mink—a wonderful little predatory animal with a characteristic odor. But if we keep *that* in mind, the line becomes an olfactory horror. It's some fusty little cave these two have in the absence of father and mother. And *their* absence takes away the real drama from the situation. It's a roll in the hay, and nothing more.

Allow me another I love:

> I.N. spells IN.
> I was in my kitchen
> Doin' a bit of stitching.
> Old Father Nimble
> Came and took my thimble
> I got a great big stone,
> Hit him on the belly-bone.
> O.U.T. spells OUT.

Here we see how light "i" and short "i" and feminine endings can make for speed, rhythmical quickness, and velocity, and then, with the words following the action, that truly awesome and portentous line with its spondees, "I got a great bíg stóne . . ."; and then the sudden speed-up in the action—the triumphant release from a frustration, I suppose the Freudians would say—"Hit him on the belly-bone./O.U.T. spells out."

Take another, a single line, which is always a test:

> Great A, little a, bouncing B.

There are three shifts of pace—it's a triad again, lovely alliteration, the long full vowels combined.

Names themselves can be a love—and half the poem:

> Julius Caesar Pompey Green
> Wore a jacket of velveteen.

73

What's my real point by these little examples? It's this: that, while our genius in the language may be essentially iambic, particularly in the formal lyric, much of memorable or passionate speech *is* strongly stressed, irregular, even "sprung," if you will. Now we see that the name itself, the direct address, makes for the memorable, for rhythmical interest; often it makes for an implied dialogue. Take the ridiculous:

> Oh father dear, do ships at sea,
> Have legs way down below?
> Of course they do, you goosey you,
> Or else how could they go?

But you may protest, these are the rhythms of children, of folk material, strongly stressed—memorable perhaps, but do they appear in poetry today? The answer is yes, certainly in some poets. For instance, Auden's:

> The silly fool, the silly fool
> Was sillier in school
> But beat the bully as a rule.
>
> The youngest son, the youngest son
> Was certainly no wise one
> Yet could surprise one.
>
> Or rather, or rather
> To be posh, we gather,
> One should have no father.

Then the cryptic and elliptical end:

> Simple to prove
> That deeds indeed
> In life succeed
> But love in love

74

And tales in tales
Where no one fails.

Not all Mother-Goosey to be sure. And the "rather-father"
rhyme maybe comes from Sam Johnson's:

If the man who turnips cries,
Cry not when his father dies,
'Tis a proof that he had rather
Have a turnip than his father.

Or take an example from myself: "I Need, I Need." In
the first section the protagonist, a little boy, is very sad.
Then there is a jump-rope section in which two children
chant in alternate aggressive dialogue. Then their aggres-
sion trails off into something else:

Even steven all is less:
I haven't time for sugar,
Put your finger in your face,
And there will be a booger.

A one is a two is
I know what you is:
You're not very nice,—
So touch my toes twice.

I know you are my nemesis
So bibble where the pebble is.
The Trouble is with No and Yes
As you can see I guess I guess.

I wish I was a pifflebob
I wish I was a funny
I wish I had ten thousand hats
And made a lot of money.

> Open a hole and see the sky:
> A duck knows something
> You and I don't.
> Tomorrow is Friday.
>
> Not you I need.
> Go play with your nose.
> Stay in the sun,
> Snake-eyes.

Some of the poems I cherish from the dramatists have heavily pronounced, strongly stressed swat rhythms. They are written to be sung, or maybe danced to. Here from *Ralph Roister Doister:*

> I mun be married a Sunday;
> I mun be married a Sunday;
> Whosoever shall come that way,
> I mun be married a Sunday.
>
> Roister Doister is my name;
> Roister Doister is my name;
> A lusty brute I am the same;
> I mun be married a Sunday.

Notice that shift in the second stanza, in tone, and feeling—how it goes into another speed rhythmically.

George Peele, that wonderful poet, abounds in incantatory effects with the same propulsion. Here is the opening of a dialogue:

> Fair and fair, and twice so fair,
> As fair as any may be,
> The fairest shepherd on our green,
> A love for any lady.

And later:

> And of my love my roundelay,
> My merry, merry, merry roundelay,
> Concludes with Cupid's curse:
> They that do change old love for new,
> Pray gods they change for worse!

Repetition in word and phrase and in idea is the very essence of poetry and particularly of *this* kind of poetry. Notice how these poets can and do change the pace, and the change is right, psychologically. We say the command, the hortatory, often makes for the memorable. We're caught up, involved. It is implied we do something, at least vicariously. But it can also be very tricky—it can seem to have a factitious strength. The emotion must be strong and legitimate and not fabricated. Thus when Elinor Wylie writes:

> Go study to disdain
> The frail, the overfine,

I can't get past the first line. There is no conviction, no natural rhythm of speech. I suppose there must be an element of the startling, or the strange, or the absurd. Yeats is magnificent, often, at getting the right tone, seizing the attention:

> Call down the hawk from the air;
> Let him be hooded or caged . . .

or:

> Come swish around, my pretty punk,
> And keep me dancing still
> That I may stay a sober man
> Although I drink my fill.

77

Or Donne's

> *So, so, breake off this last lamenting kisse,* . . .

In some more serious poetry we see again how the direct
address can pull us up sharply. We are used to this in
spoken language. Maybe we hark back to the condition of
the child when we are being told. Almost invariably a dra-
matic situation, some kind of opposition, is indicated.
Thus in Charlotte Mew's:

> *Sweetheart, for such a day, one mustn't grudge the*
> *score;* . . .

Or Donne's:

> *When by thy scorne, O murderesse, I am dead,* . . .

Or the action itself can be dramatic, as in Herbert's:

> *I struck the board, and cry'd "No more;* . . .

Or the situation can be given dramatically, as in Kunitz's:

> *Within the city of the burning cloud,*
> *Dragging my life behind me in a sack,*
> *Naked I prowl,* . . .

But what about the rhythm and the motion of the
poem as a whole? Are there any ways of sustaining it, you
may ask? We must keep in mind that rhythm is the en-
tire movement, the flow, the recurrence of stress and un-
stress that is related to the rhythms of the blood, the
rhythms of nature. It involves certainly stress, time, pitch,
the texture of the words, the total meaning of the poem.

We've been told that a rhythm is invariably produced
by playing against an established pattern. Blake does this
admirably in "A Poison Tree":

> *I* was angry with my friend,
> *I* told my wrath, my wrath did end.
> *I* was angry with my foe,
> *I* told it not, my wrath did grow.

The whole poem is a masterly example of variation in rhythm, of playing against meter. It's what Blake called "the bounding line," the nervousness, the tension, the energy in the whole poem. And this is a clue to everything. Rhythm gives us the very psychic energy of the speaker, in one emotional situation at least.

But there are slow rhythms, too, for we're not always emotionally "high." And these, as any practitioner will find, are very difficult to sustain in poetry without boring the reader. Listen to Janet Lewis's "Girl Help":

> *Mild and slow and young,*
> *She moves about the room,*
> *And stirs the summer dust*
> *With her wide broom.*
>
> *In the warm, lofted air,*
> *Soft lips together pressed,*
> *Soft wispy hair,*
> *She stops to rest,*
>
> *And stops to breathe,*
> *Amid the summer hum,*
> *The great white lilac bloom*
> *Scented with days to come.*

Here we see particularly the effect of texture, especially the vowel sounds as well as the effect of the dentates, the "d's" and "t's." The first line sets the pace. It can't be said fast: "Mild and slow and young." It's a little vignette, very feminine, absolutely true emotionally—the drowsy adolescent; but the poem is not static: the girl moves, she stirs, she stops to rest, and stops to breathe. And the girl virtually embraced by the season that is part of herself.

It's nonsense, of course, to think that memorableness in poetry comes solely from rhetorical devices, or the following of certain sound patterns, or contrapuntal rhythmical effects. We all know that poetry is shot through with appeals to the unconsciousness, to the fears and desires that go far back into our childhood, into the imagination of the race. And we know that some words, like *hill*, *plow*, *mother*, *window*, *bird*, *fish*, are so drenched with human association, they sometimes can make even bad poems evocative.

I remember the first time I heard Robert Frost read, in 1930. Suddenly a line, I think it was from Shakespeare, came into his head. He recited it. "Listen to that," he said. "Just like a *hiss*, just like a *hiss*." It is what Eliot has called "the auditory imagination": the sinuousness, a rhythm like the tail of a fish, a cadence like the sound of the sea or the arbor bees—a droning, a hissing, a sighing. I find it in early Auden:

> Shall memory restore
> The steps and the shore,
> The face and the meeting place;
> Shall the bird live,
> Shall the fish dive,
> And sheep obey
> In a sheep's way;
> Can love remember
> The question and the answer,
> For love recover
> What has been dark and rich and warm all over?

Curiously, we find this primitiveness of the imagination cropping up in the most sophisticated poetry. If we concern ourselves with more primitive effects in poetry, we come inevitably to consideration, I think, of verse that is closer to prose. And here we jump rhythmically to a kind of opposite extreme. For many strong stresses, or a playing against an iambic pattern to a loosening up, a longer, more irregular foot, I agree that free verse is a denial in terms. There is, invariably, the ghost of some other form, often blank verse, behind what is written, or the more elaborate rise and fall of the rhythmical prose sentence. Let me point up, to use Mr. Warren's phrase, in a more specific way the difference between the formal poem and the more proselike piece. Mr. Ransom has written his beautiful elegy, "Bells for John Whiteside's Daughter"; I'd like to read "Elegy for Jane" on the same theme, a poem, I'm proud to say, Mr. Ransom first printed.

I remember the neckcurls, limp and damp as tendrils;
And her quick look, a sidelong pickerel smile;
And how, once startled into talk, the light syllables
  leaped for her,
And she balanced in the delight of her thought,
A wren, happy, tail into the wind,
Her song trembling the twigs and small branches.
The shade sang with her;
The leaves, their whispers turned to kissing;
And the mold sang in the bleached valleys under the
  rose.

Oh, when she was sad, she cast herself down into such
  a pure depth,
Even a father could not find her:
Scraping her cheek against straw;
Stirring the clearest water.

> My sparrow, you are not here,
> Waiting like a fern, making a spiny shadow.
> The sides of wet stones cannot console me,
> Nor the moss, wound with the last light.
>
> If only I could nudge you from this sleep,
> My maimed darling, my skittery pigeon.
> Over this damp grave I speak the words of my love:
> I, with no rights in this matter,
> Neither father nor lover.

But let me indicate one or two technical effects in my little piece. For one thing, the enumeration, the favorite device of the more irregular poem. We see it again and again in Whitman and Lawrence. "I remember," then the listing, the appositions, and the absolute construction. "Her song trembling," etc. Then the last three lines in the stanza lengthen out:

> The shade sang with her;
> The leaves, their whispers turned to kissing;
> And the mold sang in the bleached valleys under
> the rose.

A kind of continuing triad. In the last two stanzas exactly the opposite occurs, the final lines being,

> Over this damp grave I speak the words of my love:
> I, with no rights in this matter,
> Neither father nor lover.

There is a successive shortening of the line length, an effect I have become inordinately fond of, I'm afraid. This little piece indicates in a way some of the strategies for the poet writing without the support of a formal pattern—he can vary his line length, modulate, he can stretch out the line, he can shorten. It was Lawrence, a master of this sort of poem (I think I quote him more or less exactly) who said, "It all depends on the pause, the natural pause." In other words, the breath unit, the language that is natural to the immediate thing, the particular emotion. Think of what we'd have missed in Lawrence, in Whitman, in Charlotte Mew, or, more lately, in Robert Lowell, if we denied this kind of poem. There are areas of experience in modern life that simply cannot be rendered by either the formal lyric or straight prose. We need the catalogue in our time. We need the eye close on the object, and the poem about the single incident—the animal, the child. We must permit poetry to extend consciousness as far, as deeply, as particularly as it can, to recapture, in Stanley Kunitz's phrase, what it has lost to some extent to prose. We must realize, I think, that the writer in freer forms must have an even greater fidelity to his subject matter than the poet who has the support of form. He must keep his eye on the object, and his rhythm must move as a mind moves, must be imaginatively right, or he is lost. Let me end with a simple and somewhat clumsy example of my own, in which we see a formal device giving energy to the piece, that device being, simply, participial or verbal forms that keep the action going:

BIG WIND

Where were the greenhouses going,
Lunging into the lashing
Wind driving water
So far down the river
All the faucets stopped?—
So we drained the manure-machine

For the steam plant,
Pumping the stale mixture
Into the rusty boilers,
Watching the pressure gauge
Waver over to red,
As the seams hissed
And the live steam
Drove to the far
End of the rose-house,
Where the worst wind was,
Creaking the cypress window-frames,
Cracking so much thin glass
We stayed all night,
Stuffing the holes with burlap;
But she rode it out,
That old rose-house,
She hove into the teeth of it,
The core and pith of that ugly storm,
Ploughing with her stiff prow,
Bucking into the wind-waves
That broke over the whole of her,
Flailing her sides with spray,
Flinging long strings of wet across the roof-top,
Finally veering, wearing themselves out, merely
Whistling thinly under the wind vents;
She sailed until the calm morning,
Carrying her full cargo of roses.

PART THREE

ONE RING-TAILED ROARER
TO ANOTHER

In Country Sleep and Other Poems, by
Dylan Thomas. New York: New Directions.

HAS THE RING-TAILED ROARER BEGUN TO SNORE? THE LIMP
spirit of a Peruvian prince taken over his wild psyche? Has
he shoved down the throttle only to find a ramshackle
model of patch-work fancies fluttering to a short cough?
What time's the train of his true spirit due? To what
wonders are we now exposed?

I say: The swish of his tail's wakened another wind.
The times he has stood in the white presence, the muse
blowing through him with the true fury! Behold him
now, a snout in the sun, father and mother imploring!
Long may he wallow.

But ah, where the light is, strange forms of life gather; and what creeps come after him from the cracks, their hard eyes glittering, not lovely like mice, but beetles and toads even God would like to forget: those sea-weevils winding their slimy fingers about him, carrying out his laundry and then hiding it,—May the muse spit in their ears!—those loathly wearers of other men's clothing, those ghleuphs, ouphs, oscars, lewd louies; yahoos and vultures hovering over dead and live horses; hyenas of sensibility; serpentine swallowers of their own slimy tails; dingle-dangle dilly-boys; anglo-saxon apostles of refinement; aging coy sibyline co-eds; makers of tiny surprises; tweed-coated cliché-masters; grave senatorial language-swindlers; freak monsters with three frankfurters for toes; sleazy flea-bitten minor mephistoes, playing with the Idea of Good and Evil,—May he blow them all away with a single breath! And I give them another curse: May they be condemned forever to a perpetual reading of their own works.

What he wants is another Love: the far Son in his eye, not a thick Sunday of white thighs. So he babbles and laughs out of a shrewd mouth, the mournful daughters with him spilling the seed of his soul, praying lovers together in a wordy original song. Holy supposes come out of his mouth and nose. He's bald where it suits the sun; a home-made halo he has in a sour country where at least they love a bard. And sing! O the chances he takes with the womanly words as we all wish and cry Never enough of this. Suppose he does beat the last breath from a lively meaning, he never escapes from himself without giving us more than we'd ever dare ask. Was it him I saw step from a cloud, alone as a lark, singing the things we can never know, taking a bird's grace and the breath from us, speaking and thinking with his rude flesh, not a man slowed to a walk,—as if pigs could sing and as God's spy he weeps for us all? Need such a Promethean keeper of fire and secrets look to his meanings, learned and tactful as Wystan? Should we love what we have and not wish for another thing? Here's a great master of sweating who runs and rumbles in and out of his own belly, no staid husband of the dry sad disciplines.

This rare heedless fornicator of language speaks with the voice of angels and ravens, casting us back where the sea leaps and the strudding witch walks by a deep well. May he live forever in those black-and-white dreams, a centaur of something more than he knows, while the white maidens peep from behind the hedges and all the juttiest ends begin talking at once. In a light time the tempter's wrong,—flesh from another dream, ghost on a thorn or high stone, a wonder a wave out far; a full-blown bladder in love, close to shining, the father and son of a smile.

But I say: In him God is still poor.

Wherefore, mother of fair love and the speckled hen, attend him in this hour. Angel of true serenity, nestle in his nerves. May this motion remind him of rest. His help is still in him, more than a trance of voice or skin. In sleep, in country sleep, he comes to believe.

DYLAN THOMAS: ELEGY

IT IS DIFFICULT FOR ME TO WRITE ANYTHING, STUNNED AS I am, like many another, by the news of his death. I knew him for only three brief periods, yet I had come to think of him as a younger brother: unsentimentally, perhaps, and not protective as so many felt inclined to be,—for he could fend for himself against male and female; but rather someone to be proud of, to rejoice in, to be irritated with, or even jealous of. He was so rich in what he was that each friend or acquaintance seemed to carry a particular image of him: each had his special Dylan, whom he cherished and preserved intact, or expanded into a figure greater than life: a fabulous aging cherub, capable of all things. I think Thomas often knew exactly what each person thought him to be, and, actor that he was, would live up to expectations when it suited his mood. Often this would take the form of wry, ironical, deprecatory self-burlesque: as if he wanted to remind himself of the human condition. Like Chaplin, whom he loved, he could laugh at himself without being coy, and call up tenderness in those who rarely felt it.

The demands of his body and spirit were many; his recklessness, lovely. But even his superb energies felt the strain, I should say, on lecture tours when he was set upon by fools. Any kind of social pretentiousness disturbed him, and particularly in academia. The bourgeois he did not love. And he could, and did, act outrageously, on occasion, snarling from one side of his mouth to a gabbling faculty wife that nobody ever came to America except to get fees and drink free liquor; only to wish, wistfully, the next five minutes, to someone he respected, that he could stay in this country for a time, and maybe even teach: show the young what poetry really was. But even in black moods, his instinctive sweetness and graciousness would flash through. More than any other writer or artist I know, he really cared for and cherished his fellow men.

I first met him in 1950, in New York. John Brinnin had written twice that Dylan Thomas wanted to meet me. I found this hard to believe, but when I came down from Yaddo in May, still groggy from my own private wars with the world, it seemed to be so.

Someone had lent me an apartment uptown; he was staying downtown on Washington Square. We sometimes alternated: one would rout out the other, different days. He had been built up to me as a great swill-down drinker, a prodigious roaring boy out of the Welsh caves. But I never knew such a one. Some bubbly or Guinness or just plain beer, maybe; and not much else. We would sit around talking about poetry; about Welsh picnics; life on the Detroit river, and in Chicago (he greatly admired *The Man with the Golden Arm*); the early Hammett; and so on. Or maybe bumble across town to an old Marx Brothers movie, or mope along, poking into book shops or looking into store windows. One night he insisted I come along, with others, when some fellow Welshmen, in America for twenty years, entertained. And then I saw what he meant to his own people; to those hard-boiled businessmen Thomas was the first citizen of Wales, and nothing less.

Sometimes he would recite,—and what that was many know; but I think off stage he was even better, the rhythms more apparent, the poems rendered exactly for what they were. I remember he thought "After the Funeral" creaked a bit at the beginning: that he had not worked hard enough on it.

He had a wide, detailed and active knowledge of the whole range of English literature; and a long memory. I noticed one day a big pile of poems,—Edward Thomas, Hardy, Ransom, Housman, W. R. Rodgers, Davies, and others,—all copied out in his careful hand. He said he never felt he knew a poem, what was in it, until he had done this. His taste was exact and specific; he was loyal to the poem, not the poet; and the list of contemporaries he valued was a good deal shorter than might generally be supposed.

He was one of the great ones, there can be no doubt of that. And he drank his own blood, ate of his own marrow to get at some of that material. His poems need no words, least of all mine, to defend or explain them.

RICHARD SELIG

THESE PRINCES OF LIFE LIKE SELIG HAVE A HARD TIME OF IT.
The Grecian-Hebraic profile, the dark hair, the charm
that can be turned on and off like a faucet—these qualities
can undo them, and they know it. And few people I have
met were ever more aware of themselves and the effect
they created than Selig. And it would be the worst sort
of sanctimonious cant to make him out as something he
was not. His own derisive laughter from the shades would
haunt us all, I am certain.

For he was a "crook," a real predator, a barracuda, who
could, and did, live on what he seized; who seethed with
aggression—against society, against his friends, male and
female, against, of course, himself. And like all true

thieves, he usually knew exactly what he could get away with.

Once when we were both in our cups at an ex-G.I. houseboat party, I thought he went too far in his contempt for some of the more naïve people present, and I gave him a mild, glancing poke in the jaw—the only time I have ever struck a student. He hit me back, somewhat less mildly, and then the usual virtuous fellows intervened.

But the effect was salutary. From then on, Richard condescended to no one, in class at least, and indeed often went out of his way to defend some hapless innocent in the cockpit of a course called "The Writing of Verse."

His verbal gifts, particularly in analytical criticism, were considerable; his self-assurance, staggering. And his capacity for work, when he thought it important, was enormous. For me he usually did not one but several examples of any set assignment. And no one honored the imagination more than Richard Selig.

All this, it must be understood, is about the pre-Oxford Selig, for I never set eyes on him after I left Seattle for New York and Europe in 1952.

It was characteristic of Richard that the only request he ever made of me—to write in his behalf for a Rhodes scholarship—came via a woman we both had known for a considerable time. This arrived while I was visiting my mother, in Michigan. I grumbled and raged to her—my only audience: "Why can't he ask me himself, instead of putting the squeeze on me this way?" "But maybe he's too proud to ask you," she said mildly. "I'd write the letter—you're not that busy."

So I spent the better part of a day drafting a candid but, I would like to think, eloquent letter, and that night my sister typed it. My chief and final point was this: "The British won't come it over Selig."

And the British never did. It took the high gods and an anarchy of cells to do him in.

And I relate this last incident because I think it would please Richard to know that an old and ailing woman, whom he had never seen, spoke up in his behalf. It would please him because, beneath the mask of bland cunning and ferocity,—all too frightening and real,—was a tender and compassionate man who might have become one of the fine ones of his generation, to say the least.

LAST CLASS

NOTE. In some American progressive colleges for women, it is the custom to tell all, to shoot the works, in the last class. The school here is, let us say, Hysteria Hall; the course, The Writing of Verse.

MY SINS ARE NOT IMPORTANT. WHATEVER I SAID WAS TOO good for you. I tried. I said and I did. I survived. I have endured you, O modern girl, sweetheart of papa and billboards; footpad and assassin. Lord, I'm plumb tuckered out lugging these hunks of pork up the lower slopes of Parnassus, knowing all the time that as soon as I turn around, back they'll slip to blurbanity, inanity, and the dearest, dullest people in the world. I'm tired of being a day-laborer on this canary-farm, a ladies' maid in a seminary of small beasts, a mid-wife sweating to effect a most particular parturition: bringing forth little maimed ends of life, poems with all the charm (if they didn't lay eggs) of aborted salamanders.

I'm tired of tippy-toe tasting; peripheral twittering; sniffing for epiphanies; whistling after Wystan; Tate- and text-creeping; dithering over irrelevant details; orphic posturing; adjective-casting, nuancing; mincing before mirrors; speaking the condition of somebody else's mouth; crooning in private over garbled quotations; sucking toes already too tired; attitudinizing, all those dreary glazed varnished effusions from the boudoirs of frou-frou; all the lower case freud and joyce (Anna Livia Dribblenose); all those moldy little sublimations emitting nothing more than a faint sad smell; those cats and trees and silvery moons; those bleak black ugsome birds—why not a whole series on the grave, darling? I'm tired of the I-love-me bitches always trying to keep somebody off balance; Park Avenue cuties who, denied dogs, keep wolfcubs named Errol Flynn, or bats and toads with names like Hoagy; all the cutsey, tricksy trivia and paraphernalia with which the stupid and sterile rich try to convince themselves they aren't really dead.

A young girl, said Montherlant, what a dreary subject for a writer. And don't I know it now, me up to the armpits in quivering adolescent entrails, still trying to find something I can save. Take it from me that's been hit over the head, still slug-nutty from those long years in the technique mines. I'm beginning to feel the mould creep over the noble lineaments of the soul. O the lies I've told my own energies trying to convince myself I was teaching you *something!* Twenty times a day I asked myself: Are you really worth it? And the more I asked, the more I lathered, vomiting before Thursday classes, chasing after examples like a greasy stackrat, learning passages by heart only to forget them when I got there, beating my off-stage beat to death, schmalzing all day long,—a high-speed pitch artist, a sixteen cylinder Mr. Chips, wide-open Willie (Just look sad and he'll change the assignment),—I ask you, is that the way for a grown man, and me past thirty-five, to make a living?

I shudder to think of the bromides I've bellowed; the horrendous affirmations; the immense and mindless sense of surprise with which I've belabored the obvious: all that passionate readjusting of platitudes we call progressive education. And by what garments of praise (trimmed with self-pity) haven't I lived and had my being: "Cecily-Ann says you're simply *divine* on Hopkins. I do so want to take you sometime!" Or papa, beaming with beatific bestiality that comes with a hundred grand a year after taxes: "Why, we spent a fortune on psychiatrists, but you really seem to have fixed her up." Buster, I fixed her better than you think: it just may be, in spite of everything, you have a human being on your hands who'll do something more than shake those greasy curls in the cribs of Greenwich Village.

And now, small-fry sadists that you are, you still insist on extracting the ultimate hot-flash, the last tired gasp from this semester-end throe of exasperation. In other words, I simply must say what I think of my colleagues,— as if you didn't already know us better than the backs of your hands; as if you haven't been playing us off, one against the other, watching those ever-so-slight facial flickers for some hint of a rift, some revelation to relay in Commons: "Oh, I know he *loathes* Secondary Source! He practically told me so today in conference. And as for Stinky Retriever!—"

The Faculty! Those privileged participants in this great

educational experiment, those members of a community that so honors the creative it just sucks it right up bones, blood and all. That menagerie of fly-blown lesbians, tired refugees, grass-roots Americans with classic tastes, Bonwit Teller tough guys, drama boys, saxophone players, ex-bartenders, fugitives from the loony-bin; creeps, vipers, toads, critics; finks, louts, lechers, fly-fishermen, sociologists; baby-prodders, pianists; dopes, mopes, co-ed trolls, nine-day wonders; sibyls, second-cousins, toads, hacks, trimmers; pikes, dikes, perch and bull-heads; drearies, queeries, vealy-faced fairies; strange little women full of ticks and ethics; existentialists with wet hands; sad-eyed determinists; a professor; stoolies, droolies, ninnies, bibble-babbling informers; poops and prophets.

But give them credit: most of them,—coonie and wide, obtuse, or just plain nutty,—at least aren't dull. Fond of flourishing themselves before the devil, verbal about everything except what they really know, given to thin pipings or furious bull-roarings about the secrets of life,—their desperations, their exaltations are most lavish. They can't play bridge. What they know they know to beat hell: and they care enough to give out,—by some means; twists, grunts, blasts, pokes, shrugs; off-the-cuff; on-the-snatch; down-the-hatch; or with-the-club-dinner. They are teachers.

But there are a few sour specific instances, and we *do evolve* with rather horrifying speed and in spite of all the trumpeting and snorting and parading of the ego, on and off the podium, into certain well-defined, easily discernible types. For instance, there is:

The Creep. A critic. Of the Waltz-me-around-again— Heinie, I-hear-you-calling-Cleanth school. Surprised at an early age, by polysyllables. Mad for myths and schemata. Couldn't tell a poem if it came up and bit him in the behind. A small talent for arranging ideas; an ear like a meatgrinder. There are always these coarse-faced detractors, these busy little men who bite the creative because it is human, debase the genuine truths, and emasculate the language. They pad through the halls, these insults to mediocrity, their eyes coming to alight only when salary increases are mentioned. They have ideas very publicly, these dreary bores with their clatter-language. And how they keep track of each other!

The Quince. Should have been a pimp or a cardinal's secretary. Stream-lined for Jesus, he. Ambition: to compose a great prayer. This God, of course, busy as He is, will never permit. A walk-softly who some day will understate himself into spiritual anemia: he'll prolong the moment of contemplation until it reaches a perfect psychic vacuum. His boot-licking is a marvel to behold: the least possible waste motion.

Bullo, the Barber-Shop Mystic. A lingo-bingo boy, up-high and happy. A great roaring sensibility on the loose: all ear and no forehead. Writes prose. Loves the Heartland. In winter lives on silage. Listen when he takes off.

Bufflehead. A pale, limp worm of a man, kind to his mother, considerate of his students, beastly to himself. He doesn't *know* and he doesn't know he doesn't,—that's his tragedy. Poor dear, he's going to be shunted from place to place, always preceded by marvelous letters which a year later his colleagues will re-read with astonishment. At last he'll come to rest in some backwoods academy, where except for a few embittered cynics and lazy nature boys, everybody else will be stupider than he is. Then, if he marries, he'll become an administrator.

The Udder. All gush and goodwill and guts (girth) a yard wide. A suburban Sappho. The vice in the old village choir. A mind composed largely of fuzz. If she knew what she was, there would be no harm in her, but monkey she must with every amorphous psyche that comes her way. "You can't do your assignment? Try, just try, to imagine yourself a *Tree*." But surely you classic cases in progressive pedagogy, weaned on Freud and Kraft-Ebbing, aren't taken in by such shoddy sex-transfers. What she wants, really, is to keep you entranced forever in the soft silly gloze of adolescence, to have you perpetually saying farewell to the warm womb but never once peeking out for just one look at reality. She loves you best bewildered. Let her be somebody else's mother.

The Allusionist. Do I hear "the furtive yelp of the masked and writhing poeticule"? Is this "the startling hysteria of weakness over-exerting itself"? I ask only answers. From him you can learn the pleasure of tangential authority and how never to come to the point. Even his sighs have another source. Echoes, said Hopkins, are an evil; this man is a veritable cave. And what he won't do, lack-love that he is, to keep his odious skin intact. But somehow he always survives. What's he doing, anyway, in this company of intellectual princes?

Brain Girl. The blue hair and zinc curls give you the clue, don't they? The unhappy extrovert; a female hillbilly who learned to count. So much common sense! And what crimes she commits in its name, always making the wrong decisions for the right reasons, professing a great love for ideas but actually afraid of them. A blameless public and private life; a terrible random energy. As an administrator, has done more human damage than a battalion of angels can undo. This she knows and she'll end in a fast car wound around a tree or bend double from cyanide. She can't pray: her soul has disappeared into those hand-painted jars and bottles on her dressing table.

The Raccoon. A lovely man and you know it. His prose would kill you, but, face to face, he speaks straight to the spirit. A real source of life.

But I do hear a faint well-bred sigh, a shifting of thighs that means, "Why not talk about us for a change? After all, we're the customers." And so you are dear darling provocatives.

Most exhausting, for me, are you milky sweet ones, still dimpled from mama's rosy interior, braces on teeth, straight from Miss Twitchett's or the stables of Stirrup-and-Halter Hall. Nicknames like Muffsie, Mopsy, Butter-Ball and Whim-Wham. Some of you are Irish. I can't will such willowy bones into women. I'm not a wet-nurse. What nips and bites you have, little insects for juxtaposition, delicate baby spiders already weaving webs of self-delusion. Look at you close, and invariably you'll skitter away, afraid of yourselves. Ah sweetlings, asleep in your fat, if you don't once in a while, at least look outside, the angels will be forever angry.

Then there are the self-loathers, fond of sitting on this-tles; wearers of hand-made peasant jewelry in the shape of chicken foetuses. These I have paid the compliment of thinking about in the abstract.

As for you, *Eulalea Mae*,—please rise when I name you individually and when I'm done sit down on the *end* of your spine. It's still growing, remember. From your mother, lovely blob, you inherited the serenity of a cistern. Find some suntanned idiot boy about to get an Army commission. Let him marry your belly and you'll both be happy. In the meantime avoid all language.

Pretty-for-Nice. That block you're always talking about —are you sure it doesn't fill your entire head? You don't *like* paint and are afraid of it? Try drawing with chalk in your navel. I mean: be true to your own constrictions. Get down where your obsessions are. Live with the desperate and you'll survive.

Hell-for Stuff. From me you seem to want the soft gaze of the brown bull. Alas, my dear, I'm not even a tired St. Bernard. Try a hot bath or the higher sublimations. Keep a stiff upper slip. But the caterwaul doesn't become you. That's the tom-cat's function.

Patricia Jane. In those raids on yourself you have won a few minor outposts. Now pay me the honor of writing like somebody else. I refuse to be best man at your spiritual marriage. An intense desire for experience but a horror of paying the price. To watch from a tent of mink,—that is your wish. But how well you modulate the shape of a sentence and the assonantal sounds!

Ah, true indignation! how rare you are, how dangerous to court deliberately. Have I taught out of the whole wrath? I hope I have. I know you, little unwashed beasts. I love you for what you might be: I hate you for what you are. Yes! I fried you in the right embrace: the close kiss of why not. I taught you as I should; not what I know but what I do not know. I cut you down, and left you singing in your best bones. Did I say *I*? Indeed that would be a monstrous untruth, for I was never more than an

103

instrument. But if only once or twice, some sly generous hint from the unconscious slipped from the side of my mouth, if any of you have looked for the last time into that cracked mirror of absolute self-love, then we have not failed, you and I. We both may escape the blurbs of nice, the leagues of swank and swink, all the petty malice and provincial nastiness that wants to smother, to suffocate anything human and alive.

But before I'm reduced to an absolute pulp by my own ambivalence, I must say goodbye. The old lion perisheth. Nymphs, I wish you the swoops of many fish. May your search for the abiding be forever furious. Oracular nutty's taking it on the lam. There's not enough here to please a needle. I won't say another word. I've hissed my last cliché. It's luck I wish you. Wake the happy words.

PART FOUR

REVIEWS

THE LAST LOOK AND OTHER POEMS, *by*
Mark Van Doren. New York: Henry Holt.

IN HIS FIRST FIVE BOOKS OF POETRY, MARK VAN DOREN
proved himself a careful craftsman with a sharp eye for
the homely and a mind aware of the profound implica-
tions of the casual. His best work took the form of short
"metaphysical" lyrics, durable and complete; he seldom
wrote badly. His chief influences, well assimilated for the
most part, probably were E. A. Robinson, Emily Dickin-
son, Robert Frost and the poets of the seventeenth cen-
tury. Thoroughly proficient in most of the conventional
forms, at times, like Stanley J. Kunitz and Léonie Adams,
he experimented within the tradition.

This volume is further proof of Mark Van Doren's
technical skill. In the remarkable "Private Worship," for

instance, a single metaphor is carried without a break through thirty lines to a true climax. The poem is no mere exercise in verbal ingenuity; the theme is not exhausted but enriched by the successful application of the single figure. A somewhat longer piece, "Animal Worship," and "Millennium," although impressive, creak a bit in the middle. In the simpler "Neighbor Girl" and "The Whisperer" the poet creates a heightened suspense and a haunting strangeness that are proper in variations on old ballad forms.

Some of the best pieces in the book, "Something Acrid," "The Bundle" and others, are explorations of bleak and remote corners of the American mind. The reports are more clinical than those of E. A. Robinson. Wisely, Van Doren attempts a close scrutiny of one facet of character, not a condensed life history. The approach is oblique but usually penetrating.

Yet for all the solid writing, the formal excellence, there are disturbing imperfections: monotonous verbal patterns, stanzas weakened by mannered feminine rhymes, themes overwritten. There are failures in immediacy. (Compare the title poem, for instance, with some of Emily Dickinson's on the same subject.) But the chief defect results from an ear no longer sufficiently naïve: lack of resonance. The poet who would speak in muted accents must take care that his rhythms do not falter. There is some danger that Mark Van Doren will become, like Conrad Aiken, a master of the slack line.

However, it is easy to pick flaws in the work of a truly prolific artist. Although Mark Van Doren has written no single lyric to be compared with, let us say, Louise Bogan's "The Mark," Allen Tate's "The Mediterranean" or Léonie Adams' "The Mount," the level of his achievement has been remarkably high. Perhaps in his next book he will translate more immediate experience into the intense and powerful idiom of a great lyric.

AND SPAIN SINGS: FIFTY LOYALIST BALLADS, *adapted by American poets, edited by M. J. Benardete and Rolfe Humphries. New York: The Vanguard Press.*

To read the average collection of World War poems, English or American, is a melancholy experience. Today such anthologies fill us with a sense of revulsion, and even at the time they must have been incredibly dreary. Often the sentiments were those of arm-chair heroes, the hack poetasters eager to serve the interests of the British foreign office. On one page the theme would be stand-up-and-play-the-game-for-dear-old-England and on the next kill-the-dirty-Boche. The real poems of the war—the work of Englishmen like Sassoon, Rosenberg, Sorley and Owen, the isolated examples from Americans like Cummings, the poets who put down the horror and the pity—rarely were included.

And Spain Sings, let us hasten to say, offers few parallels with such volumes. The poets of the originals and the translators are honest writers. There are no false heroics, no puerile self-glorification in these pages. Even when the poems have been written with fury and contempt, the emotions come from immediate experience and are accompanied by a fierce and often noble dignity. This is what the poets of Spain as a part of the people of Spain have written while facing the Fascist guns.

This volume had its beginning, as M. J. Benardete points out in one of the admirable forewords, when the Spanish poets, at the start of the rebellion, "revived the oldest tradition in Spanish poetry: the medieval *romance* or ballad." All of these ballads were first printed in *El Mono Azul*, the weekly newspaper of anti-Fascist intellectuals, which was founded August 27, 1936. For Spanish poetry, it was a time both good and evil: that month Federico Garcia Lorca, regarded by many as the finest young poet in any language, was murdered by the Fascists at Granada.

The methods by which the ballads were translated provide a valuable example of collective action by writers. In most instances the prose translations of editor Benardete were turned into English metrical forms; in some cases, however, French versions from the magazine *Commune* were the basis for composition. Though all the writers had the originals, as Rolfe Humphries points out, "In the strict sense of the word most of these poems cannot be called hard and fast translations; they are free versions, adaptations, paraphrase." The result is a collection in vigorous and popular language, remarkably consistent in tone, considering the number and variety of poems and translators. Poets adapt poets with effectiveness and prove that writers can cooperate internationally on a specific task.

About one third of the book is the work of Rolfe Humphries, who has turned the assonantal patterns of the originals into fairly strict stanza forms, for the most part. One of the best but least recognized of contemporary poets, Humphries has a considerable knowledge of languages, especially the classics, and a good ear for racy speech. Among his most memorable short translations are "Who Went by Here?" by Antonio Aparicio, with its effective incremental repetition; "Against the Cold in the Sierras" by José Herrera Petere; and the two ribald pieces on Mola and Queipo de Llano. But it is the long poems like Manuel Altolaguirre's "The Tower of El Carpio," Rafael Alberti's "The Last Duke of Alba," and Rosa Chacel's "Alarm!" that best show Humphries' skill. Here is the opening stanza of Alberti's poem:

> You tower-haunting martins,
> You swallows and gray doves
> Are turned to coward ravens
> Or savage vulture-droves;
> Machine guns in each cranny,
> Rifles in every niche,
> Pour on the village houses
> The blessings of the rich.

Humphries' fellow contributors, both familiar and little known, have ample chance to show their powers. Of W. C. Williams' three pieces, "Wind of the Village" by Miguel Hernandez is most interesting. Edna St. Vincent Millay puts the stamp of her style on Emilio Prado's "The Arrival." Other poets are less personal but equally moving. Willard Maas, Stanley Kunitz, George Dillon and Shaemas O'Sheel are among those who do excellent work. There are laments for fallen friends, battle incidents, praise for the brave and jeers for the despised. Rarely are the poems forced or strident, as is the case in the translation of Vicente Aleixandre's "The Man Who Was Shot."

That this volume, the work of many hands, should be so good may seem to some a fortunate accident. What has lifted even minor talents above themselves is a spirit of a great people who embody the heroic virtues of plain people everywhere struggling for a decent life. Neither these poems nor the force that has animated them will be lost on the world.

THE FIVE-FOLD MESH, by Ben Belitt. New York: Alfred A. Knopf.

There is a prejudice among a considerable section of the reading public against the book of short lyrics. Ben Belitt recognizes this attitude in the prefatory note to his first volume:

In making this selection of poems written over a period of eight years, it has been my hope to suggest a discipline of integration rather than a series of isolated poetic comments. . . . What has been sought, in a word, is an effect of sequence—a sequence which, beginning with simple responses to the natural world, moves on to an awareness of the personal identity, and attempts finally to establish usable relationships between the personal and the contemporary world.

This is an ambitious program for a book of twenty-five poems, all but three of them short lyrics. These remarks will not be so concerned with the suggested solutions as with the merit of the verse in which they are stated.

In the first three sections of his book Ben Belitt is, for the most part, the traditional lyric poet. He constructs out of a past that includes the Shakespeare of the sonnets,

Donne, Keats, and, more recently, Housman and Elinor Wylie. That "metaphysical" experience so alluring to the young provides much of the substance; the "simple responses" are made in a meticulously selected language which sometimes shows the effect of too much attention. At his worst Belitt presents the familiar spectacle of the male poet at work on his lyric embroidery: he is just another spiritual nephew of Elinor Wylie. But a firm control on his line prevents disaster even when he employs sentimental clichés like "The brown, swift girl whom we needed most," "imperious beauty," "innocent anguish."

A traditional form like the sonnet shows Belitt in typical achievement. All the examples in section II have real substance, dignity, and movement; all except the last one are just a bit mannered, even for sonnets. Perhaps a short poem like "Colophon" shows greater mastery over technique:

> In heats that drew the freshet up
> And moved in iron through the grove,
> A conscript and a burning cup
> I keep; but not in love.
>
> A harder dearth compels the word:
> It will not merge in blood or wine,
> But brims denial, like a gourd,
> And names the toast in brine.

In the central section of ten lyrics Belitt is sometimes a very young and sometimes a truly mature artist. "The Duel" is marred by attitudinizing. The basic image is archaic; the gentle hortatory cadences are boring:

> Best the ungarlanded forehead; best
> The dear contention put behind,

> The luminous arrow in the breast,
> The flowering miracle in the mind.

But in "Charwoman" and "Tarry, Delight" the poet finally breaks loose from his usual tightly constricted patterns to create poems that have the immediately identifiable mark of an individual style.

The last three longer poems—"Brief for a Future Defense" (1932), "The Unregenerate" (1936), and "Battery Park: High Noon" (1938)—are all creditable achievements. Excellence follows chronology, as it should. But the first two poems rely too much on the epithet for their effects. Once in the space of twelve short lines, twelve nouns have at least one adjective attached. In "Battery Park: High Noon" Belitt tries to see himself as poet in relation to his fellow men with that same desperateness of purpose, that same intensity of vision that was Hart Crane's. It is good to see a young poet with whatever advantages of discipline a formal education may offer attempting to carry on where Crane left off. The dangers in this attempt Belitt has not always escaped:

> Summer deploys upon the brims of hats;
> Turns upon twill; affirms with colored drinks
> A mimic solstice poised in flying inks. . . .

In the main, however, this poem is successful, especially in the final section, where the language takes on an eloquence that owes little to anyone else.

In some of his recent work Belitt effects a successful violence upon traditional language. But often he shies from the straightforward declarative statement when it would be the most powerful; he does not like the shape of a plain sentence. The best short poems are still being written by those writers who impose on themselves the strictest limitations. Such poets regard inversion as a device to be handled with extreme caution; they hate adjectives; they prefer the homely, the bald, to the decorative. Sometimes their work may be arid, but it is rarely artificial; it may be rough, but it is often powerful. And Belitt extends his suspicion of the usual beyond matters of form and style. He puts too high a premium, it seems to me, on "awareness," on being a sophisticated artist. He distrusts the good commonplace, the naïve. In so doing he cuts himself off from much of human experience. Often instead of being truly passionate, he is merely literary; he shapes ingenious verbal patterns, but they are not always poetry. Too much of his work seems to spring from an act of the will rather than from an inner compulsion. Except for half a dozen poems—and that is enough—he creates no more than remarkable artifice. In distrusting the naïve, he seems to have paralyzed at least part of his sensibility. He knows the way, but he carries too much with him.

CONCERNING THE YOUNG, by *Willard Maas*. *New York: Farrar and Rinehart*.

In his first book, *Fire Testament*, Willard Maas was a poet with a delicate eye, a highly perceptive ear, and a genuine tenderness. He was a poet at cross-purposes with himself, at times a kind of latter-day imagist, at times a writer who attempted to crack the heart of reality with the impact of abstract language. He usually survived his influences: for instance, unlike many of his predecessors, he was never content with mere snippets or fragments of observation. His poems were usually all of a piece and truly rhythmical.

Maas's second book contains much evidence of that "growth" so dear to the heart of the reviewer. A necessary transition is effected from the exclamatory to the declarative. While there is some straining for the arresting image ("Listen to the talking seconds, Liquid fire on the white tongue") usually the detail is authentic and even homely. Some excerpts from "Landward Seabirds" will illustrate Maas's quality. The beginning, replete with adjectives, reads like a parody of the early Cummings:

> The skyline
> sank green wilderness of evening
> sprouted pink clouds
> the sides
> of the building shone bright
> with sunlight
> gold the park junipers
> morning swept in from the sea
> sea blue with sky shimmer

But such water-color effects are rare. Later the nouns emerge without adornment:

> She of the whiteness
> of air-smell and lightness
> moves
> with the landscape
> the trees
> and tree-quiet

An excellent effect is achieved with feminine endings:

> the sun
> to bring singing
> the mouth has spoken
> the oars watery sweeping
>
> Bird of what waking
> and what returning
> the island
> keeping
> secrets for weeping

Frequently in this volume a love of objects purely for themselves leads to cataloguing which flattens out the poem. Though at times this seems almost a poet's note-book, such is the wealth of things observed, even the over-written pieces have interest and validity.

In his choice of forms, Maas acknowledges the modern demand for virtuosity. The more familiar patterns are almost always modified, the metronomic rhythms avoided for the most part. The longer free verse poems are competent but somewhat derivative. In some of his best lyrics he uses a short, run-on line, with occasional rhyme, half-rhyme or assonance. The first stanza of "Journey and Return" is characteristic:

> Whatever our hearts spoke
> We shall remember then:
> Pink animals of the sea
> Touched by our hands,
> The sound of the trees
> In the early morning dark
> Breaking like waves over the black land.

117

In spite of his many admirable qualities, Willard Maas remains a poet who is impressive in the body of his work but a trifle disappointing in the item. Single lyrics, with a few exceptions like "The Kind Look," "Concerning the Young," and the last two introductory poems, do not stay in the memory. Some poems, as I have said, are expanded beyond their proper size; others show evidence of being class-mangled: the machine guns, the bombs are lugged in. At times, like some of his contemporaries, Maas overworks the understatement; moreover, often a gentle irony defeats his purpose. This poet is a sensitive recorder still partly in a state of shock. Events constrict the tongue; the terror is too apparent.

All this is to be expected, perhaps, in a young writer in these times. Already a fine poet, Willard Maas in his maturer years no doubt will write fewer poems in an even sharper idiom.

THE ALERT, by *Wilfred Gibson. New York: Oxford University Press.*
GAUTAMA THE ENLIGHTENED, by *John Masefield. New York: Macmillan.*

There is a war on and an older poet of honorable talent is moved to do his duty. One expects from Mr. Gibson's title, if not the deep insight into the human heart of a Wilfred Owen, at least some of the drama, the humor, the psychic terrors of civilian life in England today. Instead Mr. Gibson gives us understatement reduced to inanity in "The Lorries," "The Whistling

Boy"; banal irony in "The Birch"; or, in "The Herd,"
analogies in the Georgian manner:

> Like a bunch of stubborn steers
> That the drover strives in vain
> To chivvy down a twilit lane,
> Baulking, whisking round again,
> Sore-beset by unknown fears—
> So the wild thoughts in my brain
> In these latter desperate years,
> Harried by the switch of pain,
> Plunge and check in an insane
> Panic as the darkness nears.

There are few lines or single phrases to give immediacy
to most of this heavy-footed pedestrian verse. One can
only be grateful that the poet never evokes hatred: this
is the work of a decent man. Yet decency is not enough,
for poetry requires, at the very least, a disciplined mind
and a truly passionate heart.

One of the characters in a play by John Masefield says,
". . . for all my wickedness I cared for truth and beauty
and color; three things which never let man down." In
his latest volume of four longish poems these noble ends
serve Mr. Masefield himself none too well. "Shopping
at Oxford," an heroic-couplet paean of praise, includes
even

> that fragrant cave
> Of joys of life and guards against the grave;
> When, besides drugs, the buyer carries home
> The sponge that sluices and the soaps that foam,
> Throat-blessing gargles, and the scented, nice,
> Pungent, sub-Tropic, cuttled dentifrice. . . .

The binder, the baker all get more than their due; there is just a bit too much of the English brand of cloying place-name sentimentality, a glozing over of the surfaces of life. What is needed is the painter's eye and sharp unsentimental mind of a Louis MacNeice at his best.

"An Art Worker" is a twenty-page account of the innocent London pleasures of a young model (to Mahlstick Tubes, R.A.) and her artist lover. The worthy Tubes is briefly mentioned:

> When he has bathed and dressed,
> His Wife is newly gowned,
> His shiny car comes round.
> Himself glossy and shiny,
> In expectation of dine-y
> With cocktail of sherry wine-y.

This excerpt does not misrepresent the quality of the whole poem; and "Mahdama's Quest," an ancient legend, has its own nightmarish badness. At least in the title poem nobility of theme gives the language a curious archaic solemnity.

Mr. Masefield, by publishing such inconsequential work, obscures many a good poet in the public eye, in publisher's office, and on library shelves. And he may well lead the uncharitable to think that, for all his early vigor and color, he has been living through a prolonged emotional adolescence. A poet, young or old, has no worse enemy than his own bad poems.

A Lost Season, by *Roy Fuller. London: The Hogarth Press.*

A good many of the poems in Roy Fuller's third volume were written while he was with the Fleet Air Arm in East Africa. They are the observations, the meditations of a sensitive intelligent man who has sufficient dignity to assume a collective guilt without seeming to be defiled. Fuller is horrified when he contemplates what he represents; when he sees what his civilization is doing to the natives of Africa. While he does not have the sense for the barbaric, the intensity of imagination of a St.-J. Perse, nevertheless he sees much, never condescends, often, I believe, renders his difficult exotic material with fidelity.

Fuller is less strident than some of his American colleagues. He rarely forces an emotion or thumps along in the familiar heavily accented five-foot line. He never postures, simpers, or caterwauls. The objective less obtrusive pieces are marked by an extraordinary vividness of pictorial detail. The whole of "The Giraffes" is memorable: the subject rendered for what it is worth, the emotion completely objectified. And "The Petty Officers' Mess," while somewhat overwritten, has a superb irony in the situation:

> The monkeys near the mess (where we all eat
> And dream) I saw tonight select with neat
> And brittle fingers dirty scraps, and fight,
> And then look pensive in the fading light
> And after pick their feet.

What gives these pieces and others like "Crustaceans" their special power is the feeling that the imagination has been forced to turn to the subhuman to sustain itself. They show, too, that a reliance on the visual image need not produce a poetry of mere surfaces. Intensely seen, image becomes symbol. The visible and invisible meet and reside in the powerfully observed.

Perhaps terms like "pictorial" or even "symbol" fail to convey the dramatic quality of the best of Fuller's work, which is evident even in the stanza quoted above. Something always happens in his external world, as it invariably does before the eyes of the true watcher. The giraffes move over the golden grass in their full and most characteristic life; or in "Crustaceans":

> At last I stretch and wave my hand: the crabs
> Instantly bolt down their holes and pull a sphere,
> A trap door, after them, and in a second
> The beach is still.

Some of Fuller's failures are technical. While he gets interesting rhythmical effects by pauses within the line, at times his ear betrays him. In general he shows too much respect for the formal stanza. The longer piece "Teba," for instance, is overstylized; the form keeps calling attention to itself. He can get verbose, or overplay his subject; he can lapse into the bathetic:

> Is it too late, too late
> For dreams to approximate?

And sometimes poems suffer from anti-climaxes or understatements that are merely flat:

> No, I will not believe that human art
> Can fail to make reality its heart.

On the other hand, the long piece "Winter in England," with its overtones from Auden and Shapiro, is best at the beginning and end, where it rises to a moving eloquence. Fuller's virtues, then, are special and his own. His less successful pieces, particularly those more deliberately willed, more "written," serve to remind us of the weaknesses in much of the poetry of our time. It is not irrelevant to note, in a more general way, what these weaknesses are, as long as we remember that Fuller's honesty of purpose and sharp eye will never permit him to write a really bad poem. These qualities give him a grip on reality which some of his even more wordy contemporaries do not possess.

For there have developed, in recent years, whole schools of verbalizers, nerveless, slick and often macabre; squeezers of the obvious, vulgar jostlers with words; cerebral gibberers and wild-eyed affirmers; helter-skelter impressionists and frantic improvisers; pip-squeak euphuists who expand a tiny emotion far beyond its proper size, who make grandiloquent pronouncements on large issues long before they have mastered the smallest of private worlds. We have listened to the gently cadenced murmurations of the sad ironists as well as to the curious yapping language, the blaring explicitness of the professionally "male" poets. We have seen gifted writers who remain satisfied with random intensities, mildly startling juxtapositions, or a few nippy local effects

The trouble probably lies in the age itself, in the unwillingness of poets to face their ultimate inner responsibilities, in their willingness to seek refuge in words rather than transcending them. The language dictates; they are the used. The cohabitation of their images is, as it were, a mere fornication of residues.

One can say that the poetry of the future will not come from such as these. Instead, it will be, let us hope, highly conscious, subtle and aware, yet not laboriously referential; eloquent but not heavily rhetorical; clear perhaps in the way Dante is clear; sensuous but not simple-minded; above all, rooted deeply in life; passionate and perhaps even suffused, on occasion, with wisdom and light.

THE EARTH-BOUND, *by Janet Lewis. Wells College Press.*

Among the women poets in this country at least three, Janet Lewis, Abbie Huston Evans, and Hildegarde Flanner, never have received their full critical due. Other writers like Marianne Moore, Louise Bogan, Léonie Adams, and some of the enterprising younger talents, have been praised frequently, sometimes for the wrong reasons or the wrong poems; but praised they have been. These three have had relatively few advocates among the reviewers and only infrequent inclusion in the more widely circulated collections of verse.

The search for reasons for such neglect, apart from the reticence of the poets themselves, leads to dreary and cynical speculation: the power of certain anthologists; the regard for what is fashionable among even the more intelligent readers; the failure of most serious critics, so

busy with text-creeping and polemics, to concern them-
selves very much with qualitative judgments in their
own time, especially regarding work that does not pro-
vide material for a particular method or habit of mind;
and so on. There seems to be no group of readers, even
among the poets themselves, that has anything ap-
proaching a catholic taste. Even the English, tired as
they are, manage, in their anthologies, to effect a kind
of rough justice to the minor or special talent.

Consequently, there is a temptation, when given a
book by a neglected writer, to correct the balance by an
uncritical "appreciation." In the case of Janet Lewis,
this is not difficult, since she is a poet who always
maintains her own tone, even in less successful pieces;
whose work is marked by an absolute integrity of spirit
and often by the finality in phrasing that can accom-
pany such integrity; whose best poems recall the tender-
ness, the pure intense feeling, the simplicity and subtlety
of early English religious poetry.

Some of her poems re-create a moment in time; in a
sense the poem is the means whereby the author escapes
from time, as in "Remembered Morning":

> The axe rings in the wood,
> And the children come,
> Laughing and wet from the river;
> And all goes on as it should.
> I hear the murmur and hum
> Of their morning forever.
>
> The water ripples and slaps
> The white boat at the dock;
> The fire crackles and snaps.

The little noise of the clock
Goes on and on in my heart,
Of my heart parcel and part.

O happy early stir!
A girl comes out on the porch
And the door slams after her.
She sees the wind in the birch,
And then the running day
Catches her into its way.

For me, the line "And all goes on as it should" has the peculiar power of summation, of drawing together experience in condensed statement that sometimes occurs in the Elizabethans. The "forever" at the end of this stanza and the last line of stanza two are a descent from this level; but the whole poem remains in the mind, fresh and immediate. Another piece, "Girl Help," achieves a fine slow rhythm without becoming fruity or over-rich:

Mild and slow and young,
She moves about the room,
And stirs the summer dust
With her wide broom.

In the warm, lofted air,
Soft lips together pressed,
Soft wispy hair,
She stops to rest.

And stops to breathe,
Amid the summer hum,
The great white lilac bloom
Scented with days to come.

Other work that can be ranked among her best includes "The April Hill," one of several elegiac pieces; the slight but charming "Lost Garden"; and some of the poems to children. "In the Egyptian Museum" has a surface excitement that for me disappears in subsequent readings: the rhythm seems wrenched; the diction over-decorative, even for the subject; the whole poem "written." "Country Burial" relies too heavily on abstractions in the opening; later after the veritable detail of the daisies that

> bend and straighten
> Under the trailing skirts

it lapses into clichés of prose:

> and serious faces
> Look with faint relief and briefly smile.

and the ending falters, it seems to me, in its effort to express too much. Possibly the theme of the poem could have been conveyed more obliquely by understatement, by detail that deepens into symbol.

But it is unfair, particularly in the work of Janet Lewis, to quote lines out of context because her poems are the sort that, in their total effect, rise above inadequate phrasing or archaic language. It is not always true that a poem is just as good as its weakest word. In these poems, sometimes the diction seems to consist of mere poetic counters, but the poem as a whole will be deeply moving, warm and luminous.

It is perhaps enough that lyric poetry be intense and passionate, however narrow in range. Nevertheless, while one is grateful for the candor, the deep tenderness and simplicity of the best of these poems, one keeps wishing that Miss Lewis would break into other areas of experience. The nursery, the quiet study, the garden, the graveyard do not provide enough material for a talent of such high order.

FIVE AMERICAN POETS

I CAN THINK OF NO REAL REASON FOR INTRODUCTIONS EX-
cept to irritate the reader into attending what is intro-
duced more closely. These poems need no words to de-
fend them.

A student of mine once wrote in an examination: "I
greet a poem, now, like a living person: with curiousity
[sic] and respect."

I suggest that if this attitude became habitual with
the ordinary reader, or even the professional critic, so
often deficient in sensibility, there would be little trou-
ble understanding most modern poetry. For curiosity
brings a certain heightening of the attention, an extra
awareness of the senses, particularly the eye and ear, an

expectancy; and "respect" means, as I take it, that the work will not be cast aside with irritation, or spurned with fear or contempt. For such a reader, the poet will be an honest man who has felt and thought deeply and intensely, or seen something freshly, and who may be lucky enough, on occasion, to create a complete reality in a single poem. Such a reader will be willing to wait for, and cherish, those moments when the poet seems to go beyond himself. Most important of all, such a reader will not be afraid of a reality that is slightly different from his own: he will be willing to step into another world, even if at times it brings him close to the abyss. He will not be afraid of feeling—and this in spite of the deep-rooted fear of emotion existing today, particularly among the half-alive, for whom emotion, even when incorporated into form, becomes a danger, a madness. Poetry is written for the whole man; it sometimes scares those who want to hide from the terrors of existence, from themselves.

Most of the poets in this group—I except Mr. Kallman with whose work and habits of mind I am less familiar— are the sort often called, rather loosely, "intuitive." Certainly all are alike in that they have not abandoned emotion. Usually they begin from within: the original impulse comes from the unconscious, from the "muse." They "wait"—and then subject the promptings of the intuition to the pressures of craftsmanship. They experiment, but usually within the tradition. With them, the poem, however oddly shaped or metrically rough, exists in itself, alive, an entity, complete and all of a piece.

Obviously, since writers are human, there can be no ideal instance of the purely intuitive poet (all ear and no forehead), or the completely conscious and resolute writer, at the other extreme, who moves easily through the geography and climate of ideas, witty and referential: the thinking type never at a loss for subject matter and a way to handle it. An excellent example of a disciplined intuitive poet would be Miss Louise Bogan in *Poems and New Poems;* among wit-writers, Mr. Robert Graves in his satirical pieces. But Mr. Graves, like Mr. W. H. Auden, can operate both ways. The genuine talent always surprises by doing *something else.* Thus, Mr. Dylan Thomas may think, Mr. Auden may look at things with a close as well as a far eye, and so on.

A word or two about these writers as separate identities.

Mr. Stanley Kunitz has a bold dramatic imagination that can wrest meanings from bleak and difficult material, turn even the language of science to lyrical purpose with speed and style. He has an acute and agonizing sense—not acquired from reading fashionable philosophies—of what it is to be a man in this century. He can break into truly passionate speech, as in "The Science of the Night," in rhythms that go back, I think, to the Jacobean dramatists. To my mind, he has written at least one great lyric, "Open the Gates," already published in his book *Passport to the War* (1944). These poems are his first after a prolonged period of silence.

Miss Jean Garrigue trusts her sensibility more completely than any other poet I know. And well she may, for what comes forth can be subtle and varied, as in her excellent "One for the Roses," with its complex richness in rhythm and diction sustained to the very end. She has a sharp eye for detail, and a considerable range. Sometimes I find myself wishing she would struggle harder to bring poems into a final form; but it is graceless to complain after being startled so pleasurably by such genuine metaphorical freshness.

An accomplished librettist, Mr. Chester Kallman has a varied, flexible technique which one wishes he would put to work more often. He can be blandly and supplely articulate as in "Superior Laughter," or more immediate in his deeply moving "The American Room." His *Elegy*, published in a small edition by the Tibor de Nagy Gallery (1951), is one of the readable longer poems of our time.

The very young today rarely "sing," in the lyrical outburst, the song. Mr. David Wagoner can, and does, in "Pause." He has an eye, too, as well as an ear; and what is often rare in the lyrical poet, a real awareness and knowledge of people.

Let me say that the writers in this group represent no new school or special coterie of friends. They are simply poets, writing at this time, who usually go their own way; have hearts and minds; trust in themselves and the imagination of the race. There are others, and many, like and unlike them. Let me say that, apart from myself, each of them, at least once, makes the language really come off, makes the poem happen. And for this, the ordinary reader, the sophisticated reader, the obtuse or sensitive critic, the fierce young, can have but one reaction: simple gratitude.

THE POETRY OF
LOUISE BOGAN

TWO OF THE CHARGES MOST FREQUENTLY LEVELLED
against poetry by women are lack of range—in subject
matter, in emotional tone—and lack of a sense of humor.
And one could, in individual instances among writers of
real talent, add other aesthetic and moral shortcomings:
the spinning-out; the embroidering of trivial themes; a
concern with the mere surfaces of life—that special prov-
ince of the feminine talent in prose—hiding from the
real agonies of the spirit; refusing to face up to what ex-
istence is; lyric or religious posturing; running between
the boudoir and the altar, stamping a tiny foot against
God; or lapsing into a sententiousness that implies the

133

author has re-invented integrity; carrying on excessively about Fate, about time; lamenting the lot of the woman; caterwauling; writing the same poem about fifty times, and so on.

But Louise Bogan is something else. True, a very few of her earliest poems bear the mark of fashion, but for the most part she writes out of the severest lyrical tradition in English. Her real spiritual ancestors are Campion, Jonson, the anonymous Elizabethan song writers. The word order is usually direct, the plunge straight into the subject, the music rich and subtle (she has one of the best ears of our time), and the subject invariably given its due and no more. As a result, her poems, even the less consequential, have a finality, a comprehensiveness, the sense of being all of a piece, that we demand from the short poem at its best.

The body of her complete poetic work is not great, but the "range," both emotional and geographical, is much wider than might be expected from a lyric poet. There is the brilliant (and exact) imagery of her New England childhood; there is also the highly formal world of Swift's Ireland; the rich and baroque background of Italy called up in the evocative "Italian Morning." And, of course, her beloved Austria. Her best lyrics, unlike so much American work, have the sense of a civilization behind them—and this without the deliberate piling up of exotic details, or the taking over of a special, say Grecian, vocabulary.

Invariably these effects are produced with great economy, with the exact sense of diction that is one of the special marks of her style. Even out of context, their power, I believe, is evident. Thus, in "Hypocrite Swift," a curious tour de force which incorporates many actual phrases from Swift's Journal to Stella, there suddenly occurs the stanza:

> On walls at court, long gilded mirrors gaze.
> The parquet shines; outside the snow falls deep.
> Venus, the Muses stare above the maze.
> Now sleep.

For one terrifying instant we are within Swift's mind, in eighteenth-century Ireland, sharing the glitter, the horror and glory of his madness.

Again, from the poem "Italian Morning," the lines:

> The big magnolia, like a hand,
> Repeats our flesh. (O bred to love,
> Gathered to silence!) In a land
> thus garnished, there is time enough

> To pace the rooms where painted swags
> Of fruit and flower in pride depend,
> Stayed as we are not.

The "garnished" and the "painted swags" are triumphs of exactitude in language; they suggest the elaborate background without recourse to merely baroque diction.

This is only one, and by no means the best, of Miss Bogan's poems on time, on change, on the cessation of time. Even in her earliest work, she seems to be seeking a moment when things are caught, fixed, frozen, seen, for an instant, under the eye of eternity.

A very early piece, "Decoration," printed in her first book, Body of This Death, but not in the Collected, is,

I believe, a beginning, a groping toward this central theme:

> A macaw preens upon a branch outspread
> With jewelry of seed. He's deaf and mute.
> The sky behind him splits like gorgeous fruit
> And claw-like leaves clutch light till it has bled.
> The raw diagonal bounty of his wings
> Scrapes on the eye color too chafed. He beats
> A flattered tail out against gauzy heats;
> He has the frustrate look of cheated kings.
> And all the simple evening passes by:
> A gillyflower spans its little height
> And lovers with their mouths press out their grief.
> The bird fans wide his striped regality
> Prismatic, while against a sky breath-white
> A crystal tree lets fall a crystal leaf.

This is a vulnerable poem, in spite of certain felicities (the fine "and all the simple evening passes by," for instance). But the uncharitable might say hardly beyond magazine verse. And even though Miss Bogan disarms us with her title, the poem remains too static, not very interesting syntactically, and the final line plays upon one of the clichés of the twenties: "A crystal tree lets fall a crystal leaf." Still, the scene is looked at steadily and closely: the poem is what it is.

Another early piece, "Statue and the Birds," is already a much better poem on essentially the same theme. However, the "Medusa," printed on the page opposite "Decoration" in the first book, is a breakthrough to great poetry, the whole piece welling up from the unconscious, dictated as it were:

I had come to the house, in a cave of trees,
Facing a sheer sky.
Everything moved,—a bell hung ready to strike,
Sun and reflection wheeled by.

When the bare eyes were before me
And the hissing hair,
Held up at a window, seen through a door.
The stiff bald eyes, the serpents on the forehead
Formed in the air.

This is a dead scene forever now.
Nothing will ever stir.
The end will never brighten it more than this,
Nor the rain blur.

The water will always fall, and will not fall,
And the tipped bell make no sound.
The grass will always be growing for hay
Deep on the ground.

And I shall stand here like a shadow
Under the great balanced day,
My eyes on the yellow dust, that was lifting in the wind,
And does not drift away.

Now, what does this poem mean?—in final terms? It
could be regarded, simply, as a poem of hallucination—
a rare enough thing—that maintains its hold on the
reader from the very opening lines to the end. But we
are told some other things, with the repetitiousness of
obsession: "I had come to the house, in a cave of trees":
the house itself is in a cave, a womb within a womb, as it

were. But notice: "facing a sheer sky"—obviously the "scene" is being played against a backdrop of heaven, of eternity, with everything moving yet not moving— "the bell hung ready to strike."

Then the terrifying moment: "the bare eyes," "the hissing hair," of the anima, the Medusa, the man-in-the-woman, mother—her mother, possibly—again "held up at a window," "seen through a door": certainly feminine symbols. And notice, "the stiff bald eyes, the serpents on the forehead formed in the air"—in erectus, in other words.

The last three stanzas bring us the self-revelation, the terrible finality of the ultimately traumatic experience. I shan't labor the interpretation further, except—why "yellow dust"? To me, it suggest the sulphurous fires of hell, here under the sheer sky of eternity.

I suggest that this is a great lyric and in an area of experience where most writers are afraid to go—or are incapable of going.

Miss Bogan is a contender, an opponent, an adversary, whether it be the devouring or overpowering mother, or time itself. And she can quarrel with her daemon, her other self, as in "Come, Break With Time." Here she manages with great skill the hortatory tone, the command, from which so much bogus poetry often results.

> Come, break with time,
> You who were lorded
> By a clock's chime
> So ill afforded.
> If time is allayed
> Be not afraid.

I shall break, if I will.
Break, since you must.
Time has its fill,
Sated with dust.
Long the clock's hand
Burned like a brand.

Take the rocks' speed
And Earth's heavy measure.
Let buried seed
Drain out time's pleasure,
Take time's decrees.
Come, cruel ease.

Notice the remarkable shift in rhythm in the last stanza, with the run-on lines that pick up the momentum of the poem. We are caught up in the earth's whole movement; I am reminded, perhaps eccentrically, of Wordsworth's

No motion has she now, no force;
She neither hears nor sees;
Rolled round in earth's diurnal course,
With rocks, and stones, and trees.

In this instance, I feel one poem supports, gives additional credence, to the other.

Yet Miss Bogan does not rest with that effect. There is a terrible irony in "Let buried seed / Drain out time's pleasure." Then the acceptance that all humans must make: "Take time's decrees." The last line remains for me a powerful ambiguity. Is she like Cleopatra, or Keats, asking for easeful death, or the cruel ease of unaware-

139

ness, of insentience, of the relief from time that old age provides? There is, of course, no final answer, and none is necessary.

One definition of a serious lyric—it may come from Stanley Kunitz—would call it a revelation of a tragic personality. Behind the Bogan poems is a woman intense, proud, strong-willed, never hysterical or silly; who scorns the open unabashed caterwaul so usual with the love poet, male or female; who never writes a serious poem until there is a genuine "up-welling" from the unconscious; who shapes emotion into an inevitable-seeming, an endurable, form.

For love, passion, its complexities, its tensions, its betrayals, is one of Louise Bogan's chief themes. And this love, along with marriage itself, is a virtual battle-ground. But the enemy is respected, the other is there, given his due; the experience, whatever its difficulties, shared.

Thus, in "Old Countryside":

Beyond the hour we counted rain that fell
On the slant shutter, all has come to proof.
The summer thunder, like a wooden bell,
Rang in the storm above the mansard roof,

And mirrors cast the cloudy day along
The attic floor; wind made the clapboards creak.
You braced against the wall to make it strong,
A shell against your cheek.

Long since, we pulled brown oak-leaves to the ground
In a winter of dry trees; we heard the cock
Shout its unplaceable cry, the axe's sound
Delay a moment after the axe's stroke.

Far back, we saw, in the stillest of the year,
The scrawled vine shudder, and the rose-branch show
Red to the thorns, and, sharp as sight can bear,
The thin hound's body arched against the snow.

This, it need hardly be said, is typical Bogan: the concern with time, the setting put down with great exactitude, the event re-created and then looked back upon—the whole thing vivid in the mind's eye, in the memory. The details are no mere accretion, but are developed with a cumulative surprise and the power of great art.

Notice the oracular, almost Shakespearean finality of "all has come to proof"—and this, at the start of a poem. She announces boldly but not portentously, and we believe. Notice, too, the mastery of the epithet—the cock's "unplaceable cry," the "scrawled vine," the rose-branch "red to the thorns." And then the final triumph of the last image, upon which everything hinges. "The thin hound's body arched against the snow."

But what has come to proof? We are not told, explicitly, nor should we be. Invariably, the final experience, however vivid and exact the imagery, comes to us obliquely. It stays with us, can be brooded upon, and brought, finally, into our lives.

This obliquity, at once both Puritan and feminine, brings Louise Bogan close, despite differences in temperament, to Emily Dickinson and to Marianne Moore. None quails before the eye of eternity; their world is their own, sharply defined. If others enter it, the arrival, the meeting, is on their terms.

Many of the best Bogan poems in this vein are of such complexity and depth that the excerpt is virtually impossible, particularly since Miss Bogan often employs the single developed image with usually at least two levels of meaning. And often, within a very short space, she effects an almost intolerable tension, a crescendo in rhythm, as in "Men Loved Wholly Beyond Wisdom"; or builds up the theme powerfully, as in the remarkable "Feuer-Nacht," and then takes a chance with a generalization without losing the momentum of the poem:

> To touch at the sedge
> And then run tame
> Is a broken pledge.
> The leaf-shaped flame
> Shears the bark piled for winter,
> The grass in the stall.
> Sworn to lick at a little,
> It has burned all.

Some of her best pieces begin with the object perceived, as it were, for an instant, and the image remembered, fixed in the mind unforgettably.

However, she is not, as I have said, a poet of the immediate moment, as say, Lawrence, but of the time after, when things come into their true focus, into the resolution, the final perspective. Listen to "Roman Fountain":

> Up from the bronze, I saw
> Water without a flaw
> Rush to its rest in air,
> Reach to its rest, and fall.
>
> Bronze of the blackest shade,
> An element man-made,
> Shaping upright the bare
> Clear gouts of water in air.

O, as the arm with hammer,
Still it is good to strive
To beat out the image whole,
To echo the shout and stammer
When full-gushed waters, alive,
Strike on the fountain's bowl
After the air of summer.

For me, the opening lines are one of the great felicities of our time: the thing put down with an ultimate exactness, absolutely as it is. Perhaps the two appositives "Bronze of the blackest shade, / An element manmade" in the next stanza are a bit "written"; but "gouts of water" saves everything. Nor do I care much for the evocative outcry—and the arm and hammer image. Yet the poem resolves itself with characteristic candor. We have come a long way in a short space.

I believe this poem will stay in the language: its opening alone demands immortality. Yet it exists, too, as a superb piece of observation; as a phallic poem; as a poem about the nature of the creative act in the no-longer young artist.

In the last lines of this piece, we hear the accent of the later work: a tone of resignation, an acceptance of middle age, a comment, often, on the ironies of circumstance. Of these, I believe "Henceforth, From the Mind" to be a masterpiece, a poem that could be set beside the best work of the Elizabethans:

Henceforth, from the mind,
For your whole joy, must spring
Such joy as you may find
In any earthly thing,

143

And every time and place
Will take your thought for grace.

Henceforth, from the tongue,
From shallow speech alone,
Comes joy you thought, when young,
Would wring you to the bone,
Would pierce you to the heart
And spoil its stop and start.

Henceforward, from the shell,
Wherein you heard, and wondered
At oceans like a bell
So far from ocean sundered—
A smothered sound that sleeps
Long lost within lost deeps,

Will chime you change and hours,
The shadow of increase,
Will sound you flowers
Born under troubled peace—
Henceforth, henceforth
Will echo sea and earth.

And certainly, "Song," "Homunculus," and "Kept," at
the very least, are among our best short lyrics. We are
told:

Time for the pretty clay,
Time for the straw, the wood.
The playthings of the young
Get broken in the play,
Get broken, as they should.

And, in terms of personal revelation, "The Dream"
might be regarded as a later companion piece to "Me-
dusa." In some of these last poems, as "After the Persian,"

"Song for the Last Act," the rhythms, the music, are richly modulated, highly stylized, grave and slow. Miss Bogan is not repeating herself, but moving into another world. There is no lessening of her powers.

I find my rather simple method of "pointing out"—at which Miss Marianne Moore is such a master—has omitted or underemphasized certain qualities in Louise Bogan's work, and of necessity passed by remarkable poems.

For example, the great variety and surety of her rhythms —that clue to the energy of the psyche. Usually the movement of the poem is established in the very first lines, as it should be:

> If ever I render back your heart,
> So long to me delight and plunder,

or

> To me, one silly task is like another.
> I bare the shambling tricks of lust and pride. . . .

And she is a master of texture, yet always the line is kept firm: she does not lapse into "sound" for the sake of sound, lest the poem thin out into loose "incantatory" effects. Thus:

> Under the thunder-dark, the cicadas resound

or the grave rhythm of

> The measured blood beats out the year's delay

or in "Winter Swan":

> It is a hollow garden, under the cloud;
> Beneath the heel a hollow earth is turned;
> Within the mind the live blood shouts aloud;

145

> *Under the breast the willing blood is burned,*
> *Shut with the fire passed and the fire returned.*

Louise Bogan rarely, if ever, repeats a cadence, and this in an age when some poets achieve a considerable reputation with two or three or even one rhythm. The reason for this is, I believe, her absolute loyalty to the particular emotion, which can range from the wry tenderness and humor of "A Crossed Apple" to the vehemence of "Several Voices Out of a Cloud":

> *Come, drunks and drug-takers; come, perverts*
> *unnerved!*
> *Receive the laurel, given, though late, on merit;*
> *to whom and wherever deserved.*
>
> *Parochial punks, trimmers, nice people, joiners*
> *true-blue,*
> *Get the hell out of the way of the laurel. It is*
> *deathless*
> *And it isn't for you.*

This, for me, incorporates the truly savage indignation of Swift—and still manages to be really funny. And even in a poem on a "high" theme, "I Saw Eternity," she can say:

> *Here, mice, rats,*
> *Porcupines and toads,*
> *Moles, shrews, squirrels,*
> *Weasels, turtles, lizards,—*
> *Here's bright Everlasting!*
> *Here's a crumb of Forever!*
> *Here's a crumb of Forever!*

I have said that Miss Bogan has a sharp sense of objects, the eye that can pluck out from the welter of experience the inevitable image. And she loves the words, the nouns particularly, rich in human association. "Baroque Comment" ends:

> Crown and vesture; palm and laurel chosen as
>   noble and enduring;
> Speech proud in sound; death considered sacrifice;
> Mask, weapon, urn; the ordered strings;
> Fountains; foreheads under weather-bleached hair;
> The wreath, the oar, the tool,
> The prow;
> The turned eyes and the opened mouth of love.

But let us see how this side of her talent operates when she is absolutely open, as in the deeply moving elegy "To My Brother":

> O you so long dead,
> You masked and obscure,
> I can tell you, all things endure:
> The wine and the bread;
>
> The marble quarried for the arch;
> The iron become steel;
> The spoke broken from the wheel;
> The sweat of the long march;
>
> The hay-stacks cut through like loaves
> And the hundred flowers from the seed;
> All things indeed
> Though struck by the hooves
>
> Of disaster, of time due,
> Of fell loss and gain,
> All things remain,
> I can tell you, this is true.

> *Though burned down to stone*
> *Though lost from the eye,*
> *I can tell you, and not lie,—*
> *Save of peace alone.*

The imagery in some of the last poems is less specific, yet still strongly elemental; we have, I think, what Johnson called the grandeur of generality. They are timeless, impersonal in a curious way and objective—not highly idiosyncratic as so much of the best American work is. Her poems can be read and reread: they keep yielding new meanings, as all good poetry should. The ground beat of the great tradition can be heard, with the necessary subtle variations. Bogan is one of the true inheritors. Her poems create their own reality, and demand not just attention, but the emotional and spiritual response of the whole man. Such a poet will never be popular, but can and should be a true model for the young. And the best work will stay in the language as long as the language survives.

EPILOGUE

A TIRADE TURNING

I THINK OF MY MORE TEDIOUS CONTEMPORARIES:

Roaring asses, hysterics, sweet-myself beatniks, earless wonders happy with effects a child of two could improve on: verbal delinquents; sniggering, mildly obscene souser-wowsers, this one writing as if only he had a penis, that one bleeding, but always in waltz-time; another intoning, over and over, in metres the expert have made hideous; the doleful, almost-good, over-trained technicians—what a mincing explicitness, what a profusion of adjectives, what a creaking of adverbs!

—And those life-hating hacks, the critics without sensibility, masters of a castrated prose, readers of one book by any given author (or excerpts thereof), aware of one kind of effect, lazy dishonest arrogant generalisers, tasteless anthologists, their lists of merit, their values changing with every whim and wind of academic fashion; wimble-wamble essayists; philosophers without premise, bony bluestocking commentators, full of bogus learning; horse-faced lady novelists, mere slop-jars of sensibility

—And those rude provincial American classicists, thumping along in a few clumsy staves, congratulating themselves in every other poem on their spiritual fortitude, their historical perspicacity, their ineffable god-like integrity; only-I-hear-it miniature Yvors, their sound effects usually the harsh rasp of a cracked kazoo; graceful anachronisms, trapped in one wavering collective image; again maundering Wordsworthians, becalmed in dear William's Sky Canoe, throbbing back into the caves of cold dismay; timid Coleridges, swallowing seconal, sucking at greasy reefers or dead cigars; undelightful bower birds wafting their faint quavers to enraptured sophomores; peripheral twitterers, their toes turned inward

—Two-dimensional dreamers: barnyard mystics, braying for eternity; Jesus-creeping somnambulist converts, clutching their rosaries, slobbering over fake Arab bones, unaware of anyone else, living or dead

—The duchess of could-you, would-you, with her acrid asides and her lady's maid diction. (When I think of her, God thickens my tongue.)

—The professionally sincere; slug-nutty nihilists; misty-moisty mush-mouthed muttonheads; Arthur Saltonstall Robinson Flubb, IV; Henry Mortimer Clift, V; Miniver Cheevy Minsky, composer of salutes to space needles and astronauts; whistling ogres; metaphysical wailers; purveyors of tired literary ham-and-cheese, gefülte fish, dead bananas; crazy rhapsodical lady poets running between religious retreats and national bridge tournaments; suburban Sapphos, decked out like female impersonators, leaning over the podium, dugs a-droop, moaning, barking like sea-lionesses

—And that breathless bounding moon-faced bourgeois bully-for-you boy, beaming idiotic goodwill from every oily pore, blowing and billowing silly bromides, belching baked beans, inane homilies, inept praises, fake epiphanies, revelling in gracelessness, obtuse awkwardness, all wrong about everything that matters, mutters, or farts in a parcel

—And the professionally insane, stepping in and out of the madhouse as others would out of their baths, happy with their half-literate therapists, condemned out of their own mouths, self-indulgent, uncharitable, insentient

—And what of the Dylan-adorers, white-eared, fawn-eyed, fervent? Or the two-bit cisatlantic tough guys making like Marlon Brando on a motor-scooter, Edna St. Vincent Millay on a raft, Rupert Brooke in a balloon, Robert P. Tristram Coffin on a blueberry muffin?

O bottom hot-cake, O hesitant pretzel,
O mile-high meringue, O prodigious pudding,
O caperer in the Kangaroo Room,
O poet of the fire-plug, the privet-hedge, the second floor,
    the back porch, the decayed brothel, the English Institute,
—O maimed waif of change!—
Was it reading you I first felt, full in my face, the hot
    blast of clatter of insane machinery?
Yet heard,

Beneath the obscene murderous noises of matter gone
    mad,
Whose grinding dissonance threatens to overwhelm us all,
The small cry of the human?

I, the loneliest semi-wretch alive, a stricken minor soul,
Weep to you now;
But I've an eye to your leaping forth and your fresh ways
    of wonder;
And I see myself beating back and forth like stale water
    in a battered pail;
Are not you my final friends, the fair cousins I loathe and
    love?
That man hammering I adore, though his noise reach the
    very walls of my inner self;
Behold, I'm a heart set free, for I have taken my hatred
    and eaten it,
The last acrid sac of my rat-like fury;
I have succumbed, like all fanatics, to my imagined
    victims;
I embrace what I perceive!
Brothers and sisters, dance ye,
Dance ye all!